STAR+GATE
Keys to the Kingdom

STAR+GATE
Keys to the Kingdom

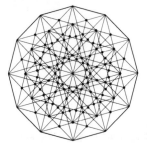

by
Richard H. Geer

Edited by
Donald Koue

Introduction by
Carolyn Myss

STARGATE ENTERPRISES

ISBN 0-911167-03-X

Published by
StarGate Enterprises
P.O. Box 1006
Orinda, California

Second Printing
February, 1986

Cover Illustration:
Frank Carson Design, Inc.
Brooklyn, New York

Acknowledgments

Although I may have the fortune of having my name placed on this book and on the other parts of STAR+GATE, there were many people who assisted in its development and progress. The joy of discovery and the pains of birthing STAR+GATE were primarily mine, yet this has always been a project that attracted the interest and talents of many. So many were involved, in fact, that it would be impossible here to list and thank them all. Each of you know who you are, and whether your contribution was major or small, I thank you for what you did. Each of you gave selflessly, and together our efforts made STAR+GATE a reality. You have my sincere gratitude.

R.H.G.

Introduction

STAR+GATE may well help you to direct the course of your life. Or it may provide a level of assistance for you in understanding a personal relationship or in moving through a professional crisis. You may ask, "How can STAR+GATE do that? It looks like a game."

And it would not be inaccurate to describe STAR+GATE as a game, for it has all the elements which comprise a rather sophisticated, delightful form of entertainment. Like many other games, it has cards (96 to be exact) and a game board. But the object of this game is dramatically different from any other you will ever possess.

Simply put, the board (the Circle Pattern) is a map of consciousness — orderly, patterned and yet unlimited in its possibilities. And the designs on the cards represent the symbols most commonly recognized by the human subconscious. Formally, these symbols are called archetypes — or original patterns from which all things of the same nature are represented.

A player forms a question in his mind, shuffles the cards and then lays them down according to the STAR+GATE Sky Spread. Three cards represent the energy of the past or literally, the background of a given circumstance. Three other cards represent the energy forming around future events, and four cards are used to represent the present moment.

Once the cards have been laid in place, the player is directed through a process of interpretation — one which involves both sides of these unique cards. The picture side of the cards evokes hunches and impressions from the player, and the word side triggers rational associations and certain levels experienced in personal situations. Interpretation also entails building creative and self-revealing pictures, and this leads to a plan of action for improving or resolving the personal topic.

Completing this stage of the game, the player positions the cards by number to their corresponding points on the Circle Pattern map of consciousness. At this point, the object is to use the map as a guide which directs the player to the elements or energy a situation lacks and/or requires in order to bring it to completion.

Providing directions on how to use STAR+GATE, however, is not the same as providing an explanation as to why STAR+GATE works and where the game originated. And while it may not be necessary for the player to understand the background of STAR+GATE in order to use the tool, the explanation will enhance for some the effectiveness and authenticity of its abilities.

In order to describe why STAR+GATE works, it is appropriate to discuss, though briefly, the more traditional tools of divination.

* * *

Tools of divination have been a part of mankind's history since man first turned his eyes toward the heavens and pondered on the nature of his existence. Every society which has ever existed — and indeed continues to exist — has been concerned and fascinated by the pursuit of its place in the scheme of the Universe.

From the Egyptian society came the earliest design of what was to become the Tarot system of divination — a series of 78 cards bearing a combination of occult and archetypal symbols. An individual skilled in the interpretation of these cards can glean a level of understanding about the energy surrounding events yet to occur or about elements of a situation not necessarily obvious to the naked eye. To master the Tarot system often requires the study of the Cabala, astrology, numerology and other schools of ancient and occult wisdom.

The East produced the I Ching. An individual seeking guidance throws three coins six times, noting the manner in which the coins fall (face up or face down). A possibility of 64 combinations of hexagrams exist in this system, each one representing a written piece of wisdom. The underlying belief is that the energy — or consciousness — of the individual tossing the coins determines the manner in which they fall.

Thus, guidance is the result of a combination of the energy of the moment plus the consciousness factor of the individual. The particular hexagram which is thrown directs the individual to the appropriate written text which holds the answer to his question.

Astrology, numerology and the Cabala are equally powerful tools of divination. Mastering any one of these systems requires, at the very least, a working knowledge of the other two systems for all three are intimately connected.

One could also say that all of these systems of divination are from the same source of consciousness in that they reflect a pattern which is an intrinsic part of the human experience — the discovery of who we are and why we were born.

All three of these tools, for example, have in common the manner in which the individual approaches these schools of divination. The Tarot system, astrology, numerology as well as the other systems assume that the person using them is seeking external guidance and direction. That is to say, the individual believes, either consciously or subconsciously, that the natural order of the Universe somehow contains the keys to unlocking the mysteries of an individual's life path. To the extent that one is capable of interpreting the natural design of the Universe, such as the planetary system or reducing the cosmos to a numerical order, then the greater meaning underlying the "natural order" of one's life can be revealed.

How does STAR+GATE fit into these ancient systems?

Perhaps as the *NEXT* step, for STAR+GATE is future oriented. The individual who uses STAR+GATE should not seek the ancient reference points, for while there are a few threads which tie this tool to its predecessors, the power of STAR+GATE is totally connected to the individual experience.

Whereas the ancient tools required, appropriately, years of study to master and often the skill of one fully schooled in the arts, STAR+GATE encourages the belief that we have reached the point along the path of human evolution where we can independently pursue a system of guidance relative to the needs of our own individual paths.

Where did STAR+GATE originate?

STAR+GATE is the creation of a man, Richard Geer, who was able to recall with a strong sense of clarity the reason he was born. In one sense, he was able to remember a form of an "agreement" made with the nonphysical world before his physical birth. The early years of his life gradually activated the memory of this purpose, and the result culminated in the development and perfection of STAR+GATE.

Richard's life may well speak of patterns to come within the design of the human experience, in which each individual's purpose is revealed with greater clarity through the inner channels of the human consciousness.

Richard is not unique, he just happens to be a pioneer clearing one more path to the inner self, or inner kingdom. STAR+GATE may well trigger each person's understanding and memory of his own purpose in life, or it may provide guidance for issues of a much smaller order. Its uses are as unlimited as life's choices, and thus STAR+GATE can be applied to any number of questions.

One element will always remain constant in the use of STAR+GATE, however, and that is no matter the issue, the source of truth is found in the discovery of your own higher self. STAR+GATE offers you the opportunity to discover the keys to your own kingdom.

Caroline Myss
Walpole, New Hampshire
February, 1984

Ms. Myss is the former founder and editor of the magazine EXPANSION, published both in the USA and in England; Vice president and Editor of Stillpoint Publishing; holds a M.A. in Psychology and Theology; specializes in research and writing in areas dealing with spirituality and patterns of mysticism within the human experience.

Contents

I
THE GUIDE

THE TURNING ABOUT

The turning-about is upon us,
the turning of mind, the expansion of eyes,
the presence of children who bathe
in the light of the stars;
their distant brothers move closer,
cherish the light that shapes from within.
Our heritage,
the spirit who soars,
the mind that dreams,
the heart that reaches out.
O, children of creation, the island of light
is within you.
As you reach for your home in the Sun,
the lamp of your becoming
strikes brilliance everywhere —
you are free.

Richard H. Geer

Introduction To The Symbolic Cards

As a tool, STAR+GATE is beautiful to look at, but, like a tool, its value lies in its use. In this section, you will be introduced to the cards and to how to use them on the Sky spread and on the Circle Pattern. Even if you have used STAR+GATE before, you will find much new information here.

Of special help is a "case study" of Ann, a young working mother with two children. Her analysis of her STAR+GATE cards is given in this section and you will find it useful in learning how to analyze your own STAR+GATE cards. From her experience you will realize, hopefully, that while there are steps to follow in STAR+GATE, the answers depend on you, on your knowledge about yourself. You will learn, too, that STAR+GATE is a flexible system. There are different ways to use it and various levels to reach. The choice is always yours. As you work through this section, you will find the ways that are best for you, just as you will find that STAR+GATE greatly enhances your own intuition about yourself.

There has never been a set of cards quite like those of STAR+GATE, and they merit a brief introduction.

Each of the ninety-six cards contains five elements — a number, a name, a picture, a Card Type symbol and a series of words. Each element expresses a facet of the overall symbol. The number shows where the symbol fits into the system, its place within the Circle Pattern. The name of the card evokes mental associations, both rational and intuitive, because a simple name can remind one of everyday things as well as connect with deep-seated, subconscious realities.

The picture on the card is intended to stimulate both conscious and unconscious associations, connections that are seldom rational in nature yet are real in their own right. The words are presented to stimulate the more rational and structured search for meaning, where the impact of the words is reviewed and weighed one by one. There is a formula or style to the word series for each type of card which will become apparent with use.

The Card Type symbol denotes the group of cards to which the symbol belongs. It expresses the level of approach of the card, a factor that adds to the overall meaning.

All the elements, through their own form, point to what the card *can* mean to the user. But it is through the process of interpretation that the player develops his or her own specific meaning, based on personal viewpoint and the situation being explored. No card has any strict meaning, and any card can have multiple meanings, all valid, for a particular player. It all depends on how the player sees the symbols in terms of himself or herself, and this can vary greatly over time and circumstances.

An analysis of each card, in alphabetical and numberical order, can be found in Section II. These descriptions can help you find the meaning for you of each card in a given situation.

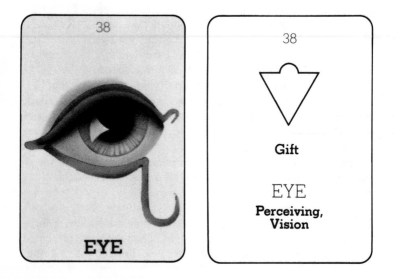

Using The Cards And Sky Spread

If you are new to STAR+GATE, before you set out to use the cards, it is suggested that you take a few minutes to look carefully through the deck. Most of the symbols are simple, but there is a great variety to them. Some people, for one reason or another, never see certain symbols in their own spread arrangements, so it is a good idea to see all that is possible before you begin.

CHOOSING YOUR TOPIC

STAR+GATE creates a symbolic picture about a specific topic that is chosen by the player. Everything that you will see in a particular spread arrangement will relate specifically to the topic you select. Therefore, it is important to be clear about what it is you want to know.

The subject you choose to explore can be anything that matters to you, anything that you want insights about. It can be a serious topic or one chosen more for the fun of it. It can be about an everyday matter or about a long-term situation. The topic can be highly specific or rather general in nature. It is suggested that the topic *not* be expressed as a question. The woman who wants to know "Should I marry Tom?" will get clearer insights into the matter if she chooses something like "Marrying Tom" as her topic. In this way, she will receive a symbolic picture about getting married and hopefully make up her mind from what she discovers, rather than expecting the cards to tell her yes or no. In fact, in this example, the primary concern might be the woman's desire to stay single. Therefore, her topic might better be "Staying Single."

Choose your own topic as clearly and simply as you can. Try to express it in just a few words, possibly writing it down to refer to.

SHUFFLING AND DEALING THE CARDS

Keeping your topic in mind, mix or shuffle the entire set of cards. Do this in any way that is most comfortable to you. It is suggested that the cards' picture side be face-down or away from you, to minimize any conscious recognition of cards while shuffling. When you feel the cards are thoroughly mixed, put them in a neat stack in front of you, still picture side down. Cut the deck, putting the bottom pile on the top of the deck. (With a new set of cards, be especially thorough in shuffling. The cards in a new deck are grouped in numerical order, which means that each card type is grouped, the way a new set of playing cards has all four suits in order.)

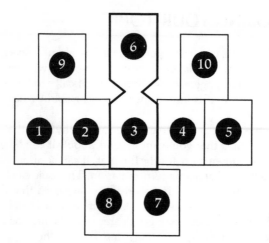

Draw the top card off the deck and place it *picture side up* in the box numbered "1" on the Sky spread. Draw the next card off the top and place it, again *picture side up*, in the box numbered "2" on the spread. Continue, drawing the next card off the deck, placing it in the box numbered "3" and so on until each of the ten boxes is filled with a single card. Any reversed cards should be turned to face you, and all ten cards should show picture side up.

You are now ready to interpret the cards. Choose either of the ways given below, the simple method or the more thorough Six-step Process of Interpretation that follows it.

INTERPRETATION—
THE SIMPLE METHOD

Start by looking at the card on the Sky spread in the box labeled THE ISSUE. The card in this box symbolizes what is at issue in you about the topic you chose to examine. It is not meant to stand for the topic itself, but rather to reveal what the reason is, what the point is, what you are trying to deal with in terms of your topic. Look at the picture on THE ISSUE card, and look at the words on the word side. Consider how the symbol indicates an issue, by freely associating with the picture and related words. Consider, too, the type of card it is, shown on the card's word side. A brief description of the Card Types is given at the end of this section. To help you discover the card's meaning, you might say to yourself, "In terms of my topic, what is at issue is like a (name of card) ."

Next, look at the card below THE ISSUE, in the box labeled YOU NOW. The card in this box symbolizes where you are right now, in terms of the topic, *and* in terms of the card that is THE ISSUE. Consider, again, the picture on the card, the related words on the reverse side, along with the Card Type of the symbol. You might say to yourself, "In terms of my topic, I appear like a (name of symbol) ."

Look at the HELPING and DISTRACTING boxes, and in the way described above, discover the meaning of the symbols in those boxes. You might say, "What is helping me is like a (name of symbol)." "What is distracting me is like a...." The term DISTRACTING indicates an influence that, in terms of your topic, is taking your attention away from the matter, is counterproductive in some way. It may appear to be a positive influence, but in terms of your specific topic it is distracting you from dealing with things.

Now look at the two boxes labeled BEHIND YOU. The symbols that are there help explain how you got to the present point in your situation. They also explain how the YOU NOW symbol came to be what it is. Look at the pictures, words and Card Types of these cards and try to discover their meaning. And again, you can say, "In terms of my topic, what is behind me is like...." Above those two symbols is the box labeled OLD FOCUS. The card in that box symbolizes an old focus of attention, a prior reason or issue that helped shape the past of the topic being examined.

Similar to the cards in the past are the two marked AHEAD OF YOU with the NEW FOCUS. The symbols in the boxes labeled AHEAD indicate where things are headed, *based on* where things are right now (as symbolized by the ISSUE and YOU NOW cards). The NEW FOCUS indicates a future issue or reason within which the AHEAD symbols occur. Any future is flexible and depends on how we deal with matters in the present.

In reviewing the cards — pictures, words and Card Types — you should come to some conclusions and insight about the topic you are examining. If you are a new player, you will also have a feel for the way STAR+GATE works and how it can benefit you.

For subsequent topics, you can get more out of the cards by trying the Six-step Process of Interpretation which is explained in the following section.

THE SEVEN CARD TYPES

STARS — ENERGIES, moods, atmospheres that surround you.

STATES — CONDITIONS, environments, states of things.

STAR-CROSSES — SELF-EXPRESSIONS, ways of acting, ways of being perceived by others.

GIFTS — TALENTS, abilities, skills.

KEYS — CHALLENGES, REALIZATIONS, confrontations about living.

GATES — ATTITUDES, approaches, ways of dealing with situations.

SIGNS — FULFILLMENT, ways of feeling satisfaction.

THE SIX-STEP PROCESS
OF INTERPRETATION

What follows is a process designed to give you the maximum value from the cards, using the Sky spread. Each part of the process is different and involves using your mind in different ways. Some parts may seem unusual or confusing at first. But try the process as it is presented; each step can unlock valuable answers inside you. And remember that you have the ultimate choice in deciding what the cards mean for you and how to make use of your insights in your life.

STEP 1 — FIRST IMPRESSIONS

After you have shuffled and dealt the cards onto the Sky spread (explained earlier in the Guide), the first thing to do is discover your own first impressions about the cards you got.

Leaving the cards picture side up, look at each card in each labeled box. In each case, see if you have any instant recognitions of why certain cards showed up in certain places. Which cards seem very appropriate to you and your topic, and which ones don't? Which cards make you feel good, and which bad? Try to get in touch with your own reactions as you look at every card. Don't worry about resolving the situation you are exploring at this point, but do take the time to make note of your first impressions.

STEP 2 — EXPLORING THE WORDS

Next, turn all the cards over to the word side. Explore the words related to each symbol, but also take into account the Card Type of the symbols. Card Types are shown on the cards' word side in colored symbols. There are seven types in all, and they represent various levels of approach involved in personal situations.

Look at the distribution of the Card Types in your spread arrangement. What patterns do you see? Are there symmetries, clusters, repetitions that appear? You can learn about the Card Types briefly by looking at the descriptions for them at the bottom of the Sky spread, or by reading the descriptions given at the end of the Simple Method of Interpretation (earlier in the Guide). More detailed information on the Card Types is contained in the Information section of the book. Sometimes you can learn as much about your topic from the Card Types involved as you can from the actual symbols themselves.

Go on to read and consider the words listed on each card. The words always have to do with the particular Card Type, as you will see with more use. Consider how any or all of the words on a card have to do with the situation you are exploring. You may even want to look up particular cards in this book's Information section, and find out more about certain symbols.

STEP 3 — DECIDING AND TURNING

Now that you have had your first impressions of the cards in the spread and explored the cards' word side, it is time to come to some conclusions about what each card means for you.

Start first with a card whose meaning you feel you understand. Make sure you have at least an idea of what the card is about and how it applies to your topic. Then turn the card back over, to the picture side, and let the picture serve as a reminder of what you feel the card means. Go on to another card. Conclude, as best you can, about its meaning. Turn the card back to the picture side, again letting the picture be a reminder of the meaning you have decided on. Continue through the other cards in the spread, in any order you want. Decide about the card's meaning, turn the card back to the picture side, and let the picture become a reminder of the meaning you chose. When you are finished, all the cards will be picture side up.

STEP 4 — PICTURE STORIES

This is one of the most valuable parts of the process of interpretation, but it can be difficult to do at first. You will be looking at groups of symbols in the spread and making pictures with them which will then tell a story, a revealing story about your topic.

First, look at the three cards in the area of the past, the two BEHIND YOU along with the OLD FOCUS. Let yourself imagine a single picture made up of the three symbols on these cards. Do not be concerned about what the picture looks like; just try to freely imagine *one* picture that contains the elements from those three cards.

A simple example is this: the three cards are the Chest, the Tree and the Rain. The picture might be imagined as a chest buried under a tree in the rain, and the rainwater is eroding the earth around the tree, exposing the top of the chest. Another way the same set of symbols could be seen is this I (the player) am dragging a chest along in the rain and take shelter under a tree. Notice in this example that the player involves himself as part of a picture, which can be done especially when the symbols seem inanimate.

The next part of this step is finding out what the picture means. With each of the three cards in the past, you have some idea of their individual meaning. Therefore, there is a *story* about the past of your topic contained within the mental picture you formed. Discover for yourself what the picture is saying about the past of your situation. This will help you understand what has brought the present about.

Do the same with the three cards in the future, the two AHEAD OF YOU along with the NEW FOCUS. Imagine a single picture composed of these three symbols. Once you have the picture in mind, take a mental step back. Look at the interaction of the symbols, and discover the story about the future of the situation that is contained in the picture.

Form the same kind of mental picture with the HELPING and DISTRACTING cards. How do they interact in one picture? What is this telling you about the pluses and minuses involved in your situation?

Now remove all the cards from the Sky spread except for the central cards, YOU NOW and THE ISSUE. Imagine a mental picture that contains these two symbols. This picture is the core of the Sky spread. Be open and honest in imagining what this picture looks like. Then discover the story within the picture because it is the most important of them all. It describes where you are and what you are dealing with, in terms of your topic.

No matter what your picture story was with these two cards, no matter what you thought about it, good, bad or indifferent, you can take a further step and improve the way things are.

STEP 5 — THE BEST PICTURE

In this step you will go beyond the level of insight into transformation. You will re-shape the picture and, in doing so, create a plan of action for improving your situation.

With the YOU NOW and ISSUE cards, create the best looking picture you can think of. Instead of just *imagining* a picture, here visualize one that is the *most positive and constructive* picture possible. Use just the elements of the symbols themselves, but make up the BEST PICTURE. Having created the picture, discover what it is telling you. It is a symbolic plan for how to improve things, for how the situation can better be approached, for how to act and what to do. Consider its message, what it means for you.

STEP 6 — LEVEL OF APPROACH

In Step 5, interpreting the cards was completed, but this final step, Level of Approach, can serve as a benchmark for watching change and progress in the topic you explored. It is a way to be aware of your current posture towards the situation.

Look at the word side of your YOU NOW card. Find its Card Type, then look up that type in the list below. Your Level of Approach can serve as a basis for comparison when you explore the same topic again with STAR+GATE.

> **STAR** — LEVEL OF RADIANCE — Being part of a pervading mood or atmosphere, one that affects you and those around you.
>
> **STATE** — LEVEL OF CIRCUMSTANCE — Identifying with outside conditions, giving credit to things other than yourself when things go well, blaming circumstances when there are difficulties.

STAR-CROSS — LEVEL OF EXPRESSION — Expressing yourself to the world, but with a concern for how others will see you.

GIFT — LEVEL OF TALENTS — Developing and demonstrating inner gifts, talents and abilities.

KEY — LEVEL OF CHALLENGE — Facing present issues head on and realizing that the tools for change are always at hand, though often disguised.

GATE — LEVEL OF ATTITUDE — Recognizing limiting approaches and developing and fine-tuning new attitudes.

SIGN — LEVEL OF FULFILLMENT — Feeling satisfaction and completion, yet preparing to seek new kinds of fulfillment.

THE SIX-STEP PROCESS
OF INTERPRETATION

SUMMARY OF STEPS
STEP 1 — FIRST IMPRESSIONS

Go through the cards, picture side up, getting your impressions about each symbol in each box on the Sky spread.

STEP 2 — EXPLORING THE WORDS

On the word side of the cards, explore distribution of the Card Types and consider the words on each card.

STEP 3 — DECIDING AND TURNING

Conclude about each card's meaning, turn the card to the picture side, let the picture serve as a reminder of the meaning selected.

STEP 4 — PICTURE STORIES

On the picture side of the cards, imagine combined picture with these groups of symbols, BEHIND YOU and OLD FOCUS, AHEAD OF YOU and NEW FOCUS, HELPING and DISTRACTING. As you imagine each picture, discover the story it tells. Remove all cards from the spread except YOU NOW and THE ISSUE. Make a picture with them and discover the story it tells.

STEP 5 — BEST PICTURE

Transform the picture of YOU NOW and THE ISSUE into the best possible picture, then discover the improved approach contained in the picture.

STEP 6 — LEVEL OF APPROACH

Check Card Type of YOU NOW card, to find current posture as a benchmark for progress.

USING STAR+GATE WITH OTHERS

Involving other people when you use STAR+GATE can greatly increase its benefit to you. It is both interesting and rewarding to share what you see, feel and experience. You may be surprised to learn other people's perceptions of the symbols as they relate to your own topic.

Try going through the process of interpretation, telling the other person what you are experiencing at each step. As you go, let the other person share what he or she sees. Watch for places where you have the same perceptions, and for places where they differ.

You might also choose to explore your relationship with another person, or a decision that affects both of you, or a problem that you face together. You can also use STAR+GATE twice, first from your point of view and then from theirs.

However you choose to do it, involving others can add a rich dimension to the process, while broadening the ways STAR+GATE can work in your life.

ANN'S SKY SPREAD

Ann's topic, the behavior of her six-year-old daughter, is the sort many of us have in life — a situation in which our own actions may be crucial in improving a relationship. Her daughter's behavior was not extreme or abnormal, yet there were things Ann did not like, and she wondered about her own role in the child's development. She brought the problem to STAR+GATE. In line with the advice earlier about posing the problem not as a question but as a simple statement, thus opening wide the doors of intuition instead of trying to squeeze them down to "yes" or "no" responses, Ann posed her topic as "My relationship with my daughter."

Here are the cards she received:

Ann's Sky Spread

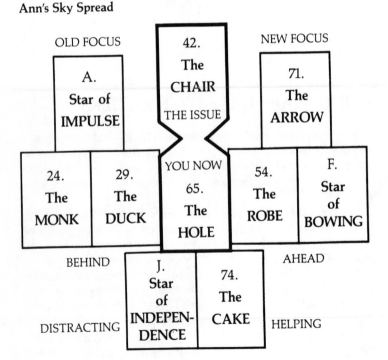

Step One — First Impressions. Ann looked through her spread of cards briefly, describing her initial impressions about each card in relation to the topic. In the area of the past, she saw the Star of Impulse as a focus representing scattered energy. It was descriptive to her of the lack of direction in their relationship and that they had just been reacting to one another. The symbol of the Monk reminded her of her daughter — uncommunicative. The Duck she saw as herself in the past, trying to make things work but floundering. All three of those symbols painted an accurate picture of how things had been.

In the area of the present, she saw the You Now card, the Hole, as very appropriate, the mother opening but directing things from her point of view. She saw the Chair as The Issue as their working together; it symbolized a place where they could both sit side by side. The Helping symbol, the Cake, she saw as a symbol of giving between mother and daughter. The Distracting card, the Star of Independence, was seen as personal pride that got in each other's way. Ahead of her, she saw the Robe as stability and calmness, and the Star of Bowing as getting along with each other, working together. Above those symbols was the New Focus, the Arrow, which she perceived as a positive direction for their relationship.

Step Two — Exploring the Words. The cards were then turned to the word side, and Ann considered both the Card Types and the words that were on each card. In doing so, she began to change her mind about some of her symbols. Discovering that the two cards Behind her were Star-crosses, she recognized that both the Monk and Duck represented divergent ways she had expressed herself in the relationship. One was very inward, the other more outward, but the result was almost two-faced. This occurred under the Old Focus of a Star that indicated undirected energy that surrounded her and her daughter.

It was very appropriate to her that the You Now card was a Gate card, indicating attitudes and approches, exactly her present concern, as well as the fact that Openness was involved. Learning that the Issue card was a Gift, Ann saw the Chair symbol as opportunity, that she and her daughter can work together and that it will take effort, give and take. Looking at the Helping card, the Cake, as a Sign or fulfillment aspect, Ann saw that give and take at the moment was more focused on rewards and physical satisfaction rather than on emotional gratification. Seeing a Star (of Independence) in the Distracting box, she viewed its energy as the desire to be apart rather than cooperate together.

Looking at the cards Ahead of her, Ann discovered that the Robe, which she had first seen as a kind of stability, was a Key or challenge card that had to do with roles. She recognized that each person's role in the relationship might well become challenging, but that it could indeed lead to realizations for both of them. The Star of Bowing (also Ahead) with its energy of Intergrating showed her that they really could create an atmosphere of cooperation. Ann saw the New Focus of the Arrow as her ability to point the relationship in the right direction through Decisiveness and Spontaneity.

Step Three — Deciding and Turning. In Ann's case, she had been developing conclusions about her cards in the first two steps, and she found it easy to express what each symbol meant. She went through the spread, highlighting each card's meaning, then turning it back to the picture side. The pictures reinforced the conclusions she had already made.

Step Four — Picture Stories. Now Ann's spread became animated and revealing as she began to play with pictures in her mind. First she looked at the three symbols in the past, the Star of Impulse, Monk and Duck. She imagined a picture of a Monk with a Duck's face under the hood and the agitated light of impulsiveness shining around the figure. When asked what she thought the picture meant, Ann answered it was like constantly being at odds with herself, a sort of Jeckyl and Hyde, not knowing how to act. To her, this truly portrayed her dilemma of the past.

Next she imagined a picture with the cards in the area of the future, the Arrow, Robe and Star of Bowing. She saw herself wearing a robe of stature, holding an arrow with the light of Integrating all around her. To Ann, this represented a personal sense of direction, of knowing how to act and making her approach fit the situation. This was the picture of how she wanted the relationship to turn out.

With the Helping and Distracting cards, she saw the Cake glowing in the light of Independence. Here, the positive and negative influences switched roles. She found the symbol of material rewards transformed by the Star of Independence into a symbol of rewards without motives. In her words the Cake now symbolized "no guilt, no strokes, just sincerity."

With her You Now and Issue cards, she saw the Chair sitting on the grass next to the Hole. To Ann, this meant an outer aspect of herself (the Chair) being in a better position to utilize her more open, inner perspective (the Hole). She liked seeing these symbols side by side, each aspect helping the other. Yet, in a way, they did not interact with each other. They just sat there, beside each other.

Step Five — Best Picture. Here, Ann had the opportunity to create the best looking picture possible, and to see what it might indicate in terms of a new approach.

In her mind, she played with the same two symbols for a few minutes, and then she announced that she had put them together. She had placed the Hole *on* the Chair, integrating the inner and outer aspects of herself. She interpreted this to mean that she could trust her inner feelings about how she should act, that she had sensed how to respond to situations with the daughter in the past but had avoided putting it all together.

She had to laugh at the fact that the picture now looked like a child's potty chair. Yet that turned out to be meaningful. Ann, as a mother, knew better than anyone else each step in her daughter's development. She knew when her child had outgrown diapers and could begin using a potty chair. And when the potty chair was mastered, the mother removed it. The symbol indicated the mother's ability to know what is best for the child and to use whatever tools are appropriate to help the child grow up. It became Ann's reminder of her role as a mother in raising the child.

Step Six — Level of Approach. Ann briefly took note of the Card Type of her You Now card. As a Gate it indicated dealing with the situation from the Level of Attitude. The emphasis was quite aptly on dealing with her own attitudes about relating to her daughter.

NOTES ON USING THE SKY SPREAD

1. Name of the Spread Early man gazed into the expanse of the night sky, most likely pondering his purpose on Earth and the nature of the universe that surrounded him. At a time that preceded recorded history, man projected his thoughts and dreams into patterns of stars in the heavens. There were his gods, his warriors and other mythic archetypes, in a library of starry patterns that returned to his view night after night. The name of the basic STAR+GATE layout was chosen as the Sky spread to tap back into that prehistoric heritage so that one might imagine the Symbolic Cards appearing out of the wonder of the night sky.

2. The Spread's Story Line The numbered boxes one through five on the spread represent a story about the player in terms of his or her topic. There are two boxes about the past (Behind You), one about the present (You Now), and two about the future (Ahead of You). The cards received in these places represent the person himself, regardless of the types of cards involved. It can be helpful to look at the story line of the spread, and to see how one symbol begins the story (#1) which leads to the next (#2) and so on, with the story ending at the box on the far right (#5). The key to the story line is always in the center, the present You Now card. What occurs in the past is only there to show why the You Now came to be what it is. Similarly, the cards in the future are there to indicate where things are heading, based on the way things are in the present.

3. The Spread's Focuses The story line in the spread actually represents the player, but the three focuses that make up the line (Old Focus, The Issue and New Focus) do not necessarily describe the player himself. These are *focuses of attention*, whether they be facets inside or outside oneself. They do not need to be seen as hard and fast parts of reality, but their reality is certainly real in the sense that one's attention is fixed on them. The terms "focus" and "issue" are almost interchangeable, also.

4. The Helping and Distracting Cards These two cards refer to the present and are not directly related to past or future. Also, they are often confusing to the player, sometimes paradoxical in nature. There may be occasions when it seems that the symbols in these two boxes should be switched, the Helping symbol seen as Distracting and vice versa. Often the process of Picture Stories helps the player understand the real role of these symbols in relation to his or her topic.

5. The Issue and You Now Cards These symbols are the key to the rest of the Sky spread, the core of the information available to the player. Every effort should be made to work with these symbols in the clearest way possible. In doing so, watch for how the two symbols interact in the Picture Story process. Does the You Now act on the Issue or the other way around? Do they avoid each other or confront each other? During the Best Picture part of the process, try to see that the You Now symbol actually does confront and deal with the Issue symbol. The picture of that action will serve as the blueprint for successfully dealing with the actual situation.

6. Making Picture Stories Doing this part of the process can seem difficult at first. The key is to actually imagine a *picture* in one's mind of the group of symbols. Often it is such an instantaneous grouping of images that the player is hardly aware he has formed a picture. Or it is one so simply conceived that the player discards it, thinking there is something better to find. It is exactly those immediate pictures, though, that are the most accurate and revealing.

Try always to stay with just the simple symbols involved, adding no other elements into the picture. The one exception is oneself, especially when the symbols all seem inanimate. In these cases, it is quite permissable to insert oneself into the picture in order to put it all together.

Working with Stars in Picture Stories can seem more difficult than with other symbols, especially when more than one Star is involved. When there is such difficulty, try looking back to the card's word side. Imagine the word that describes the Star's energy as creating a certain kind of atmosphere around the other symbols involved. Or imagine the being described on the card, like "The Doer," as actually present in the picture but invisible. When there are two or more Stars in a picture story group, try imagining either the mix of atmospheres in one place or the imaginary beings together, each wanting its own way.

THE LIGHT

"The story of the light," he said,
"is in the dance of the Stars.
Look above you, in the sky.
All the universes spin within me;
all that I am is waiting for you;
and my song is in the dance of the Stars.

"Look in every direction, and you will see
the twelve Princes.
Their glory shines among you
though their home remains in my heart.

"Come out now, my son,
and take your place with me.
See the light within the light,
the mind within the mind,
step into the dance of the Stars
that is you."

Richard H. Geer

Introduction To The Circle Pattern

After using the Symbolic Cards and Sky spread to explore a topic, you can discover more about the cards you received by plotting their positions on the map of STAR+GATE, the Circle Pattern. By doing so, you will be able to see relationships between the symbols that could not be recognized otherwise. Having the symbols translated into positions on the Circle Pattern reveals connections and relative positions leading to a clearer, more meaningful perspective on your topic.

The STAR+GATE Circle Pattern looks like a complicated web at first. Before using it, you need to understand how the various parts of the Circle fit together and interact. The short introduction that follows will enable you to read the STAR+GATE map. After that you will learn various ways to use the map. Finally, you will see how using the Circle Pattern deepened Ann's understanding of her topic and allowed her to see some surprising new meanings in her Symbolic Cards.

The Circle Pattern is dramatically different from the apparent simplicity of the Symbolic Cards, but it is important to know that the cards evolved from the Pattern and not the other way around. To truly understand the cards and the overall sense of STAR+GATE, it is beneficial to be familiar with the Circle Pattern. Once you understand the way the Circle is organized, it will serve as a ready reference for any of the deeper looks you may take at the symbols.

To begin with, imagine that the Circle is empty, no criss-crossing lines, just a center point and an outside edge. There are two enormous urges at work on the circle, the same two pervasive urges we feel throughout our living. One could be called the urge to "go home" and the other, the urge to "stay out late." They are equal and opposite inclinations, each with its own validity at different times and in different situations.

The urge to "go home" is the desire to return to a source. Dorothy had that feeling about Kansas in "The Wizard of Oz." The source is the beginning place, or wherever we were before we were here. This is what the center of the Circle Pattern represents. Wherever we may be in life, we are capable of feeling the urge to "go home," back to the center.

Balancing that is the desire to do more, to move away from the center, to "stay out late." This is the urge to go everywhere, do everything, know everybody. We can be anywhere in life, and suddenly this urge pushes us past old limits, toward the outside, beyond where we have been. Here, we feel the desire to expand, whereas the opposite is to contract.

Neither of these pulls is inherently good or bad. Certain situations can make us feel one way or another. At times we experience a sort of push-pull; one part of us wants to go home, and the other wants to stay out late.

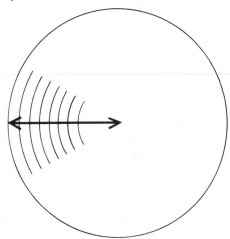

One urge pulls us inside to the inner universe, and the other brings us out, a push into the outer world. From where we live, we don't know how far inside we can go, or how far outside. So the center and the perimeter of the Circle Pattern represent absolutes, extremes we don't really expect to reach in normal life. We are always somewhere between the two, and that is the part which STAR+GATE maps.

THE SEVEN LEVELS

STAR+GATE points out seven stages between the inside center and the outside edge of the Circle. This provides a way to chart the integration of the physical and non-physical realms and of expansion and contraction in life. Looking at the Circle Pattern, you can see rings of colored points that mark the Circle at different levels. Each point represents a Symbolic Card, and the rings of colored points indicate the seven Card Types, or classes of symbols. The rings describe the spectrum of human awareness. The span is between the most deep-seated sense of fulfillment (the innermost ring of green Sign points) and the expansive, creative radiance of consciousness (the outer light-yellow Star points). In between these rings are five other levels. These include the blue ring of Gates — the psyche's postures, attitudes and approaches; the purple ring of Keys — confrontations, challenges that lead to realization; the pink ring of Gifts — unique qualities, talents and abilities; the double ring of orange Star-cross points — ways of expressing ourselves out in the world; and the deep yellow ring of States — the conditions we can find ourselves in, the tools for discovery, progress and even destruction.

THE COLORED LINES

Each color of line on the Circle represents a different kind of connection, and together they spin a web of interrelationships between the Circle's points and therefore between the symbols themselves.

Having looked at the Circle as empty, let's begin to add the lines, color by color. The blue Cloud lines emanate from twelve places on the edge of the Circle, dividing the edge into twelve segments. These segments will give us a way to distinguish one part of the circle from another, like the difference between ten and eleven o'clock. The Cloud lines also create all the major divisions *within* the Circle's area. If you look at pairs of parallel blue lines, you will see the outside limits of the twelve areas on the Circle called Houses.

Notice the long rectangles running across the Circle made by blue lines and the outside segments of the Circle. Each half of a rectangle, from the center out to the edge, is one House. Near the center of

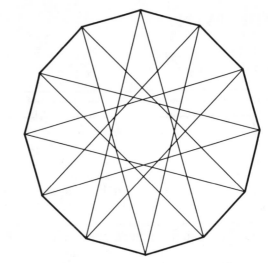

Circle's
Blue Lines

the Circle, the Cloud lines converge, creating an inner area called
the Hall of Signs. The House areas overlap one another around the
Circle, but each House can be located easily if you remember that
the top of each House is made by the outer edge of the Circle, the
sides by the blue Cloud lines, and the base merges with the Hall
of Signs at the center of the Circle.

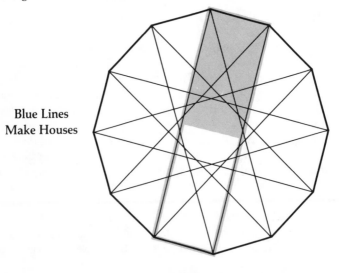

Blue Lines
Make Houses

The Cloud lines represent the most subtle kind of connection on the Circle Pattern, connection through *concept*. This can best be likened to the mind's ability to make connections and associations, to have an unchecked flow of ideas, to literally conceive of connections.

Next we overlay the blue lines with the green and see what they add to the Circle. There are two kinds of green lines.

Green Lines (Bold) over the Blue

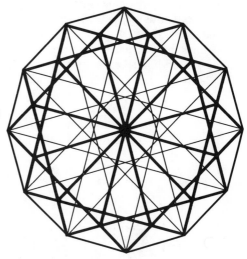

Those that emanate from the Circle's outside edges (where the blue lines begin) make large overlapping squares around the outer part of the Circle. These are called Bridges, and they represent connection through *relationship*, a kind of arm in arm connection like brothers and sisters in a ring. The other green lines, those that pass through the Circle's center, emanate from where the Bridges first cross one another. These green lines are called Lineage lines, also representing connection through relationship but, in this case, more that of parent and offspring than of siblings. The flow of the Lineage is toward the Circle's center. In each House there is a central Lineage line, parallel to the outer blue lines of the House.

Finally, we add the yellow lines over the green and blue. Although the yellow lines add much of the visual complexity to the Circle, they simply repeat the patterns already established by the other lines. Where the yellow lines start are large yellow points called Stars. You can see that the Star points form a circle within the main Circle. This circle is turned slightly, which results in each House having two Stars and each Star being shared by two Houses. The Star points are located where the green Bridge lines cross within the sharp angles, or Vs, formed by the blue Cloud lines.

The Stars (Cards marked A-L), as discussed in more detail in the Information section (II), represent essential kinds of energy. The yellow lines that emanate from them are called Star lines. Within the ring of Stars lie all the numbered points represented by the Symbolic Cards (marked 1-84). Each numbered point, or symbol, is therefore a unique mix of emanations from the Stars connected to it.

Yellow Lines (Bold)
over Green and Blue

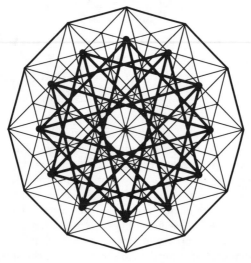

The blue Cloud lines provide subtle connection by *concept*, and they outline the basic areas of the Circle. The green Bridges and Lineages add structure through connection by *relationship*, both around and through the Circle. Now the Star lines, building on the foundation of the others, bring the map to life, providing connection through directly *experiencing,* of being, doing and encountering in order to truly know ourselves and the world.

THE TWELVE HOUSES

With an overview of how the Circle is divided, look now at the nature of those divisions, the Houses. The STAR+GATE system involves a twelve-part Cycle of Growth that describes the cycle that all things go through from beginning to ultimate completion. The cycle is applicable to the development of an idea, the life of a person, the course of a relationship, the evolution of a culture, etc. It applies to anything large or small, tangible or intangible, individual or collective.

Here is an example of the cycle in terms of human growth (words in quotations are the keywords for the Houses I-XII). "I AM." An infant just is. It lives and experiences. Its consciousness, however simple, is the center of its universe. "I WANT." An infant finds it has needs and learns to express them. "I RELATE." The emerging person sees that there is a world to deal with, things to learn about and communicate with. "I FEEL." He begins to discover himself, his own ways, styles, moods. "I PROJECT." He learns the art of expression, of playing roles. "I BECOME." He adds to himself, develops, envisions careers. "I INTERACT." He makes connections with others, establishes relationships. "I CARE." He discovers the power in uniting, the desire to be more. "I REALIZE." He uncovers his own purpose and begins to see the higher purposes for living. "I PERFECT." He improves himself and helps others to do the same. "I EXPAND." He sees beyond personality to a large scheme, accepts his limits yet reaps richer rewards. "I MERGE." He is complete, acts in step with the whole, and in doing so, dissolves back into it. He is ready for a new "I AM" at another level of being.

The arrangement of the twelve Houses is shown on the diagram below, where two opposite House areas are highlighted. It is important to be able to look at the Circle Pattern and distinguish the House areas. Remember the outer edges of each House are two parallel blue lines. The "top" of a House is the outer gold bar on the Circle, and toward the center of the Circle the House merges with the Hall of Signs area.

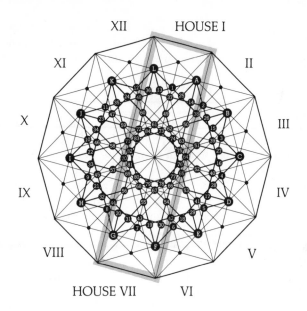

Due to the overlapping nature of the House areas, it can appear difficult to find in which House a particular point lies. Although it may seem that one point lies within the territories of several Houses, there is only one main House for each point. This becomes simpler when one is able to identify the Garden area which is located in the middle of each House.

The diagram on page 33 shows the area of one House and outlines the interior Garden structure. The pair of parallel blue lines marks the outer limits of the House. Parallel to them is a green lineage line running through the center of the House. At the top of that lineage line is a point that is shown in white on the printed version of the Circle Pattern. This point is not labeled with a number or letter like the other points, and it represents the name of the House itself, such as "I. The First Cause." Below that point, on either side, are two Star points. Below them is a figure-8 in yellow lines, symmetrical to the green Lineage line. This figure-8, outlined in the diagram, is called the Garden.

In the Garden area, the uppermost (outermost, on the Circle) point is the dark yellow State point. Below it, on either side, are two orange Star-cross points. Just below and between them is a pink

GARDEN

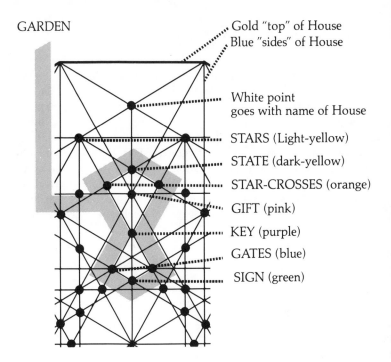

Gold "top" of House
Blue "sides" of House

White point
goes with name of House

STARS (Light-yellow)

STATE (dark-yellow)

STAR-CROSSES (orange)

GIFT (pink)

KEY (purple)

GATES (blue)

SIGN (green)

Gift point. Below it is a purple Key point, below that are two blue Gates, and finally at the base of the Garden (nearest the Circle's center) is the Sign point.

When you want to know which House a point is in, first determine which Garden the point belongs to. It is easy, then, to see which House the Garden is in. Simply follow the green Lineage line out toward the Circle's edge where the Roman numeral for the House is shown.

There are two exceptions. Star and Gate points are shared between *two Houses*. While this may cause some initial confusion, it should quickly become easy to determine which two adjacent Houses these points belong to.

The foregoing will give you the orientation needed to perform the Analysis by Houses presented later in this Guide. What follows is an entirely different way of looking at the Pattern, in terms of areas called Seas.

THE TWELVE SEAS

The Seas were a discovery about STAR+GATE that came after the original recognition of the Houses. More insight about one's symbols can be gained by having an understanding of the Sea a symbol is part of. The information below will provide the necessary background to do the Analysis by Seas described later in the Guide.

When you look at the diagram of the Circle with just the blue Cloud lines, you are able to see the twelve Houses and the Hall of Signs by seeing the blue lines creating *rectangles.* To recognize the Sea areas, you need only to look at the same blue lines as creating angular divisions — almost triangles — instead of boxes. Each of these angular areas — or Vs — is one of twelve Seas around the Circle.

The Houses can be thought of as the more masculine aspect of the Pattern, and the Seas as the more feminine side, although these

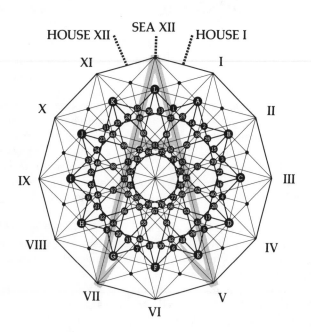

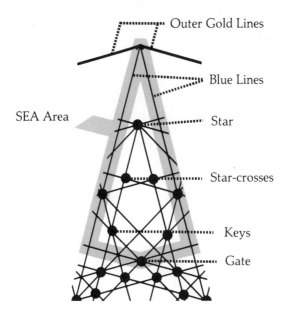

Outer Gold Lines

Blue Lines

SEA Area

Star

Star-crosses

Keys

Gate

terms are used in a broad sense and are not meant to refer to differences in gender. More to the point, the Houses are territorial, visibly organized and connec*ting*, whereas the Seas are connect*ed*, more simply organized, and act more as reservoirs within the system. One is more external, the other more internal.

The Seas also describe the Cycle of Growth but in their own way. This cycle of the Seas is explained in detail in the Information section of this book. The order of the Seas is shown in the diagram on page 34, where the twelfth Sea lies between the twelfth and first Houses. The Seas are numbered I-XII clockwise around the Circle.

The overlapping of the Seas does not present the kind of complexity seen with the Houses, so there is no special name given to the interior structure of Seas, the points connected by yellow lines. It is on the tie-shape structure that the points relevant to a Sea are found. First, at the top of each Sea is a Star, whose particular energy can be thought of as filling the Sea area. Below the Star are two Star-crosses, side by side. Below them are two Key points, which also connect to the adjacent Seas. At the base of the Sea is a Gate point. This represents the way into and out of the area. (This is why every Gate point has two words or phrases that indicate paired approaches.)

*   *   *

That ends the geography lesson. By now you should know the Circle Pattern's basic areas, the Houses, their Gardens, the twelve part Cycle of Growth, the seven Levels or Card Types, and finally the Seas. With what you have learned, you are equipped to use the Circle Pattern in deeper interpretation of the cards.

Using The Circle Pattern

This section explains four methods for analyzing symbols on the Circle — Circuits, and Analysis by Stars, by Houses and by Seas. Each method is independent of the other, each reveals something different about your symbols, and you may select any or all of the methods depending on what kind of information you find of value.

The following pages show how to perform the analysis techniques with the two key symbols from the Sky spread, You Now and The Issue. However, the methods can be used with any of the other symbols in the spread, as you wish.

CIRCUITS

Circuits is an analysis method that allows you to use the Circle Pattern to determine what other parts of yourself could be brought to bear in order to help resolve a particular topic. This technique will be especially helpful if you experienced difficulty in forming the Best Picture from the Sky spread's Six-step Process of Interpretation. Completing the Circuit, as described below, will give you one or more additional symbols to add to your Best Picture. This will result in a revised plan of action or approach that may be easier to understand and implement.

All of the points on the Circle Pattern represent parts of oneself. In truth, we all have all the parts at our disposal, but our own styles and the situations that arise tend to emphasize certain qualities and not others. Circuits allows us to call on these other, less emphasized parts of ourselves for the benefit they can bring to specific situations.

To begin with, after using the cards and Sky spread to explore a personal topic, check the number or letter of the two key cards in the spread, the You Now and The Issue cards. Find the corresponding letters or numbers on the Circle Pattern and mark these spots with a small coin or similar marker.

You can see that yellow Star lines flow through the two marked points. Star lines represent connnection by *directly experiencing* (see Introduction to the Circle Pattern), and each point has Star energies running through it. Look at the lines flowing through your two points to see if they are connected or not.

Usually the two points are not connected directly by a *single, straight yellow* line. However, if they should be, this means symbolically that they are linked by a common energy, and that they are in a relatively harmonious position to one another. If this is the case, nothing additional is indicated with the Circuits technique.

Most often, the two points are not directly connected. Symbolically, this represents the situation that warranted your utilizing STAR+GATE in the first place. In most cases, the You Now and Issue are somewhat at odds with each other; plotting their place on the Circle reveals a certain dis-connectedness.

The map can help resolve that. Look along the yellow lines that flow through your two points. Try to find one point that could be added, the result of which would be a group of three points that connect up — like part of a circuit. There are cases where it may take two additional points to create a connected group of points. There are also cases when there may be several options. When you have choices, try to choose as few extra points as possible, and choose those points that correspond to symbols that you feel are the most fitting for yourself and your situation.

Symbolically, the extra point(s) that make a circuit with your two points represent a place where relatively divergent energies are brought into a harmonious *combination* of points. This means that the Symbolic Card(s) corresponding to the point(s) is a part of yourself that can help You Now deal with The Issue.

To learn how to take advantage of this part of yourself, find the corresponding card in the deck and place it on the Sky spread along with your You Now and Issue cards. Explore the picture and word side of the card. Then re-make your Best Picture adding in its influence. This will create a revised picture that stands for a revised approach to dealing with your topic.

AN EXAMPLE OF CIRCUITS

For an example of the Circuits technique, let's look again at Ann's spread. In exploring the topic of her relationship with her daughter, Ann had received the Hole (#65) as the You Now and the Chair (#42) as The Issue. These she plotted on the Circle Pattern.

In Ann's case, there was only one simple and direct way to make a circuit; it was by the addition of #29, the Duck. Interestingly, that symbol had appeared in her spread in one of the Behind You positions.

When she had finished with the Best Picture from the Six-step Process of Interpretation, Ann had a picture of a hole placed on a chair. She had interpreted this to mean integrating the inner and outer parts of herself, a unifying that would help her deal with her daughter. Adding the extra element of the Duck into the picture re-introduced a factor that had been part of the past of the topic. (In fact, the same symbol had come up for Ann in previous spreads on other topics about herself. Dealing with a recurring symbol, Ann found, can lead to greater insight.)

Ann reshaped the picture, creating this image: a chair sitting with its legs in a hole and a duck walking around the outside. The pic-

An Example of Circuits

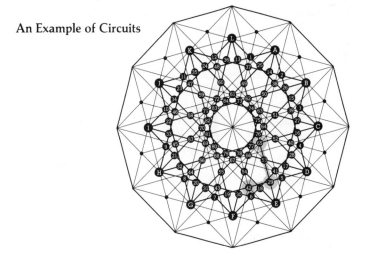

ture contained a great deal of meaning for Ann. The Duck was no longer a facade of levity that masked a more serious inner concern about the relationship. Now it represented the necessary cheeriness and naturalness that would help translate her own knowledge into actions that were more understandable to the daughter. She realized she had greeted the kind of self-expression the Duck represented with mixed emotions in the past. At times, she saw it as showing a cheerful acceptance, and at other times she saw it as indicating an avoidance of personal responsiblity. The new picture brought the symbol into a more positive light. Also, combining the chair and hole indicated a more deliberate integration of her inner and outer aspects; they were more truly combined, yet each kept its own integrity. The chair was recognized, too, as being a very necessary aspect of structure, both for her own internal process as well as in guiding her daughter.

ANALYSIS BY STARS

The Analysis by Stars is helpful in understanding the nature of any symbol. It is a way of using the Circle Pattern to identify the basic energy components that created the symbol. This analysis method can be especially beneficial when it has been difficult to see why a certain Symbolic Card occurred in a spread. The technique is explained for the You Now position, but it can be used with any symbol.

Since the yellow Star lines pass through all the numbered points on the Circle Pattern, each of those points can be seen as having been created by a certain mix of Star energies. Once a specific point is located on the Circle, the basic energy ingredients for it are found by tracing back to the Star points that are directly connected to it.

These are the steps for Analysis by Stars:

1. On the Circle Pattern, mark the point that corresponds to the number on your You Now card. (For lettered Star cards, an alternate method is given later on.)

2. Find and mark the Star points that are connected to your point by straight yellow Star lines.

3. Find the corresponding Star cards, and use the informatin on the word sides of the cards to explore how these energies interact with each other. Stars close to your point have a stronger influence than Stars farther away. Stars equally distant from your point have an equal influence.

4. Re-evaluate the idea of You Now in the Sky spread in either of two ways; a) in terms of how the different Star energies define and explain the You Now symbol, or b) look at how each of the imaginary beings listed on the cards would each deal with the symbol of The Issue.

The goal is to get a better understanding of what energies comprise your You Now symbol, and to have a better idea of how it (and its ingredients) interacts with The Issue.

EXAMPLE OF STAR ANALYSIS

In Ann's case, she looked at her You Now symbol plotted on the Circle Pattern, #65 The Hole. She noted the yellow Star lines that passed through that point, and traced back along those lines to the Star points. The Star ingredients for the Hole were:

C. Star of Change: "The Mover" — *Adjusting*
E. Star of Laugh: "The Player" — *Externalizing*
H. Star of Hope: "The Prayer" — *Trusting*
L. Star of Patience: "The Dreamer" — *Imagining*

Stars C and E were equally close, and Stars H and L were equally farther away from her point.

Ann noted that the two closer energies (Adjusting and Externalizing) were both relatively active in nature. In contrast, the pair of energies farther away were rather passive. To her, this was a reflection of the quandry she had been in about internal and external parts of herself, and at the same time it was a very fair representation of the ability to combine those two facets, both a part of the Hole. Seeing the energies involved, she saw balance between the two more active energies and between the two more passive ones as well as a balance between the two pairs. Such balance was something she

**An Example of
Analysis by Stars**

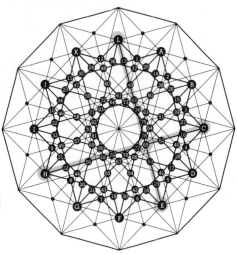

sought in herself and in the relationship with her daughter. She also noted that the slightly closer pair of energies were the more outgoing, and this helped her see that it was important to bring out of herself things that were developing within.

Ann also looked at how the imaginary beings from the cards would each deal with her symbol of The Issue, the Chair. She saw "The Mover" as someone who would move the Chair, taking control in situations that arose in the relationship. "The Player" she saw as one who would use a chair as a stage prop, as a mime might use a simple prop to act out a variety of colorful roles. This indicated spontaneity in responding to issues with her daughter. Ann saw "The Prayer" as someone who would use the chair for praying, to gather insight. Similarly, "The Dreamer" rested on the chair, shaping the dreams that would become reality.

All in all, what Ann discovered from Analysis by Stars was the formula of basic energies at work within her symbol of the Hole. Although she uncovered few surprising new facts about the topic, it gave her a more organized way to understand impressions gathered earlier.

Since the symbol of the Duck had played such a key role in her spread, Ann chose also to look at the Star formula for it.

#29. The Duck
    E. Star of Laugh: "The Player" — *Externalizing*
    D. Star of Inwardness:"The Feeler" — *Internalizing*
    G. Star of Indecision:"The Dancer" — *Weighing*
    L. Star of Patience: "The Dreamer" — *Imagining*

The Duck is a Star-cross symbol. Star-crosses are the only points on the Circle Pattern where there is an unequal series of energies. Each Star is at a different distance from a Star-cross. Therefore, there is decidedly a leading energy whose influence prevails over all the others. In the case of all the other types of points (States, Gifts. etc.), there are pairs of co-equal energies. For the Duck, E is the closest star and L the farthest.

Ann saw within the symbol of the Duck that there were two very strong influences, the Stars of Laugh and Inwardness, and that the former was clearly the dominant influence, being the Star closest to her point. This meant that "The Player's" desire to externalize, to bring it all out, always won out over "The Feeler's" desire to take it all in. She found this very appropriate to the beneficial role this symbol had taken on for her, that it was necessary to act out inner awareness. She also noted that the energy of Weighing could add hesitancy and that again the energy of Imagining was involved, as it was in the Hole. She saw that there was a personal issue of dreams versus deeds, revealed by the repetition of active and passive energies in both symbols, the Hole and Duck. But it was the key role of the Duck in revising her Best Picture (see Circuits section) that stressed the need to act more than think.

ALTERNATE METHOD
(FOR STAR CARDS)

If the point in question is a Star point, it symbolizes a basic energy ingredient, not a mix of energies. Although the above method does not directly apply to Star points, you can learn more about a Star with the following method.

Find the lettered Star point on the Circle Pattern that corresponds to your Star card, and mark it in some manner. This point will be one corner of a large square made by yellow Star lines. Find and mark the three Star points that make the other corners of the square.

The three other marked Stars play a role in relation to your Star. The energies of the two Stars that are on the corners of the large square *adjacent* to your Star can be seen as *supportive* of the energy of your Star. The energy of the Star *opposite* yours *opposes* the energy of your Star. Find the cards in the deck that correspond to these Star points. Use the cards' word side to discover which kinds of energy, moods or atmospheres are helpful to you and which is a factor that limits or checks the energy of your own Star.

ANALYSIS BY HOUSES

Analysis by Houses gives you a way to compare where the You Now symbol is on the Circle Pattern versus where The Issue is. Although it is a qualitative analysis with much left to the interpretation of the player, it allows you to see where your position is on the Cycle of Growth about a specific topic. It also shows where your own growing edge is, by pinpointing where else on the cycle your attention is focused, where the issues are in terms of a topic.

In order to use this technique, you will need to be familiar with the idea of the Houses and the Garden structure as explained in the Introduction to the Circle Pattern section.

Although the following explanation is written for the key cards in the Sky spread, the You Now and Issue, other symbols can be analyzed in the same manner.

These are the steps for Analysis by Houses:

1. Find and mark the two points on the Circle Pattern that correspond to your You Now and Issue cards.

2. Determine which Garden, and therefore which House, each point is in, and mark those Houses near the outside of the Circle Pattern.

3. Remember: both Stars and Gates are shared between two adjacent houses. In the case of those points, mark both Houses they belong to.

4. Read the descriptions about the Houses you marked (see Information Section). Compare how The Issue is in one House and the You Now in another. The House descriptions should help re-state or explain the nature of the topic.

5. Card Type or Level of Approach can also be taken into account, adding an important dimension to the analysis.

As an example of 4 and 5 above, suppose the Cup (#49) was your You Now card. Number 49 is located in House I on the Circle Pattern. The You Now has to do with one's basic self-expression; it pertains to the "I AM" part of the Cycle of Growth. Next, add in the fact that the Cup is a Key card, a challenge or realization. So You Now, the Cup, represents the challenge of "I AM." With each card you analyze this way, try to complete the following sample sentences:

The You Now card is in the ___1st___ House, and so it relates to ___"I AM ."___

The Issue card is in the ____ House, and so it relates to I_____ ."

Then build on the sentences by adding in Card Type/Level of Approach, such as this:

The You Now is a ___Key___ , and therefore it is the ___Challenge___ of "I ___AM___ ."

The Issue is a ___(Card Type)___ , and therefore it is the ___(Level)___ of "I_____ ."

Although this may seem awkward at first, learning to complete these sentences with the appropriate words will provide brief, meaningful statements about the Houses of your symbols. Below are some words related to Card Type/Level of Approach that will be of help in forming your own statements about the Houses.

TYPE	LEVEL	POSSIBLE WORDS
STAR	Radiance	radiating, the light of, the energy of
STATE	Circumstance	the condition of, the state of

TYPE	LEVEL	POSSIBLE WORDS
STAR-CROSS	Expression	expressing, the expression of, acting out, demonstrating
GIFT	Talents	the quality of, bringing out, the gift of
KEY	Challenge	the realization of, the challenge of, addressing, realizing
GATE	Attitude	the approach of, the gateway to, believing in
SIGN	Fulfillment	the fulfillment of, the completion of, satisfying

EXAMPLE OF ANALYSIS BY HOUSES

When Ann did her analysis by Houses, she plotted her two main cards, the You Now and Issue (#65 Hole and #42 Chair) and saw, by looking at the Garden areas her points were in, that The Issue was related to the sixth House and her You Now, being a Gate, was related to both the fourth and fifth Houses. The statements she formed read like this:

"The You Now is in the ___4/5th___ Houses, and so it relates to both ___"I FEEL"___ and ___"I PROJECT."___
The Issue is in the ___6th___ House, and so it relates to ___"I BECOME."___

To Ann, exploring her relationship with her daughter, this aptly described the overall situation she was experiencing. She had felt both internal and external urges, typified by the fourth and fifth Houses, and she was trying to put it all together in order to be a better mother and friend to her daughter. When she added in Card Type/Level of Approach, her statements read like this:

The You Now is a ___Gate___ and therefore it is the ___approach___ of both ___"I FEEL"___ and ___"I PROJECT."___
The Issue is a ___Gift___, and therefore it is ___bringing out___ ___"I BECOME."___

An Example of Analysis by Houses

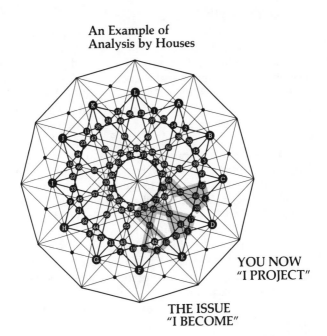

YOU NOW
"I PROJECT"

THE ISSUE
"I BECOME"

To her, this was exactly the situation, but she had never seen it so clearly stated, in a way that was simple, true and liveable.

Ann also wanted to look at the House and Level of her extra card from the Circuits technique, #29 The Duck. She found this was in the fifth House, and she made the following sentences about it:

The Duck is in the ___5th___ House, and it relates to "I PROJECT."

The Duck is a ___Star-cross___, and therefore it is the expression of "I PROJECT."

To her, this was a message that she could really trust. It seemed right — for her, for her daughter and for the relationship. The position of the Duck on the Circle Pattern looked almost like a bridge, a midway point, between where she had been and where she was headed, the key to getting from where she was to what she wanted.

ANALYSIS BY SEAS

This analysis method is much like the Analysis by Houses in that it provides a rather qualitative feel for symbols. However, the Sea areas on the Circle Pattern are far more *subjective* in nature, whereas the Houses are more *objective* aspects. Both Houses and Seas describe the universal Cycle of Growth, but the Seas speak more about the underlying qualitities of growth than about their manifestations.

Also, only certain types of points occur in the Sea areas — Stars, Star-crosses, Keys and Gates. The other types are not involved in terms of this analysis method because, with the Seas, the interior area is more significant than what lies along the borders.

The geography of the twelve Seas is explained in the Introduction to the Circle Pattern section. However, the easiest way to spot the Seas is to look at the long tie-shaped *spaces* outlined in yellow Star lines lying between the Garden areas on the Circle. Each of these is a Sea, with a Star point at its top, a Gate point at the base, and two Star-crosses and two Key points along the lines.

There are no actual steps required to perform this analysis. For any point you want to explore, such as the You Now or Issue symbols, mark the symbol on the Circle Pattern and determine the Sea it is in. Then read about that Sea in the Information section, and see what it adds to your understanding of the symbol. When plotting points in more than one Sea, you will notice relative differences in positions within the Cycle of Growth, just as you would with the Analysis by Houses technique.

EXAMPLE OF ANALYSIS BY SEAS

Ann looked at her You Now symbol, the Hole (#65), on the Circle Pattern and saw that it was a part of the fourth Sea, the Sea of Magic. Number 42, her Issue symbol, was outside of a central Sea area, and so the method was not applicable to it. In reading about the Sea of Magic, Ann took note of her own inner wealth

An Example of Analysis by Seas

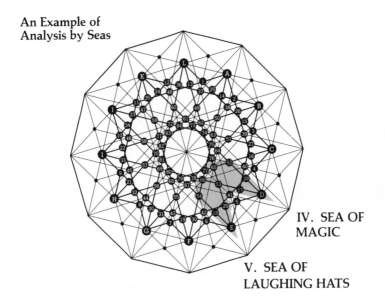

IV. SEA OF MAGIC

V. SEA OF LAUGHING HATS

of strength and knowing. She realized that the Hole, a Gate to the area, indicated access to awareness and also provided a very needed outlet, a way to release her strength and vitality and put it to work.

Ann also wanted to know more about the symbol of the Duck, and she found that it was part of the next Sea in the Cycle, the Sea of Laughing Hats (V). In reading about this area, she saw that the Duck was an expression of being in a role and enjoying it, of making the most of things regardless of the circumstances.

II
THE INFORMATION

PREFACE

This section provides descriptions of the areas on the STAR+GATE Circle Pattern, the twelve Houses and the twelve Seas, and of the points on the Circle which correspond to the ninety-six Symbolic Cards.

In order to clearly understand the nature of these areas and positions within the Circle, it is recommended that the Introduction to the Circle Pattern in The Guide section (I) be read first.

In the text that follows, the use of all capital letters or quotation marks around words refers to the key words associated with specific cards.

The Twelve Houses

I

FIRST CAUSE

I. HOUSE OF THE FIRST CAUSE

"I AM"

This area has to do with one's basic self-expression, including likes and dislikes, disposition and physical appearance.

The energies (Stars) of "I AM" are those of "The Dreamer" and "The Doer." The condition (State) is that of the Sand. The expressions (Star-crosses) are those of the Magician and the Wanderer. The Gift is in the Root, and the realization (Key) is through the Cup. The significant attitudes (Gates) are symbolized by the Tower and the Glove. Fulfillment (Sign) is the Mountain.

The Seas of Dreams and Time (XII and I) surround this Garden of "I AM."

II

MATRIX

II. HOUSE OF THE MATRIX

"I WANT"

The emphasis of this area is on resources at any level. These include pleasure, comfort, possessions and wealth.

The energies (Stars) of the Matrix are those of "The Doer" and "The Speaker." The condition (State) is that of Lightning. The expressions (Star-crosses) are those of the Lover and the Tree. The Gift is the Eye. Realization (Key) is through the Rose. Significant attitudes (Gates) are symbolized by the Glove and the Ice. Fulfillment (Sign) is the Cake.

The Seas of Time and Innocence (I and II) surround this Garden of "I WANT.

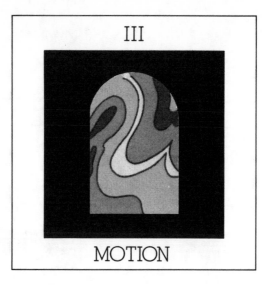

III

MOTION

III. HOUSE OF THE MOTION

"I RELATE"

This area is concerned with comparing oneself to surroundings, with gathering information, and with communicating and socializing.

The energies (Stars) of The Motion are those of "The Speaker" and "The Mover." The condition (State) is that of Rain. The expressions (Star-crosses) are those of the Child and the Chest. The Gift is the Tunnel. The realization (Key) is through the Powder. Significant attitudes (Gates) are symbolized by the Ice and the Stone. Fulfillment (Sign) is the Cross.

The Seas of Innocence and Birth (II and III) surround this Garden of "I RELATE."

IV

PURE WATER

IV. HOUSE OF THE PURE WATER
"I FEEL"

This area has to do with satisfying inner needs, with feeling secure and with one's emotions in general.

The energies (Stars) involved with The Pure Water are those of "The Mover" and "The Feeler." The condition (State) is that of Mud. The expressions (Star-crosses) are those of the Egg and the Glass. The Gift is the Harp, and realization (Key) is through the Serpent. Significant attitudes (Gates) are symbolized by the Stone and the Hole. Fulfillment (Sign) is the Sea.

The Seas of Birth and Magic (III and IV) surround this Garden of "I FEEL."

SPIRIT INCARNATE

V. HOUSE OF THE SPIRIT INCARNATE

"I PROJECT"

This area relates to how we express ourselves to others, our need to show creativity and our need for validation and praise.

The energies (Stars) of The Spirit Incarnate are those of "The Feeler" and "The Player." The condition (State) is that of Fire. The expressions (Star-crosses) are those of the Moon and the Duck. The Gift is the Circle, and realization (Key) is through the Chain. Significant attitudes (Gates) are symbolized by the Hole and the Sword. Fulfillment (Sign) is the Star.

The Seas of Magic and Laughing Hats (IV and V) surround this Garden of "I PROJECT."

VI

GRAND PLAN

VI. HOUSE OF THE GRAND PLAN
"I BECOME"

This area concerns refining what we express, making use of our energy and the kinds of work or service we perform.

The energies (Stars) of The Grand Plan are those of "The Player" and "Majesty." The condition (State) is that of the Water. The expressions (Star-crosses) are those of the Jester and the Leaf. The Gift is in the Chair, and realization (Key) is through the Robe. Significant attitudes (Gates) are symbolized by the Sword and the Token. Fulfillment (Sign) is the Lamp.

The Seas of Laughing Hats and Kings (V and VI) surround this Garden of "I BECOME."

VII

PERFECT UNION

VII. HOUSE OF THE PERFECT UNION

"I INTERACT"

The emphasis here is on involvement with others, on relationships, partners, agreements and all the ways we combine energies.

The energies (Stars) of the Perfect Union are those of "Majesty" and "The Dancer." The condition (State) is that of Earth. The expressions (Star-crosses) are those of the Maiden and the Bell. The Gift is the Letter, and realization (Key) is through the Gate. Significant attitudes (Gates) are symbolized by the Token and the Handle. Fulfillment (Sign) is the Cave.

The Seas of Kings and Music (VI and VII) surround this Garden of "I INTERACT."

VIII

POWER

VIII. HOUSE OF POWER
"I CARE"

This area represents the power that comes from combining with others, and learning the need for give and take — both within relationships and in oneself.

The energies (Stars) of The Power are those of "The Dancer" and "The Prayer." The condition (State) is that of Thunder. The expressions (Star-crosses) are those of the Butterfly and the Knife. The Gift is the Wheel, and realization (Key) is through the Wind. Significant attitudes (Gates) are symbolized by the Handle and the Rod. Fulfillment (Sign) is the Pearl.

The Seas of Music and Pyramids (VII and VIII) surround this Garden of "I CARE."

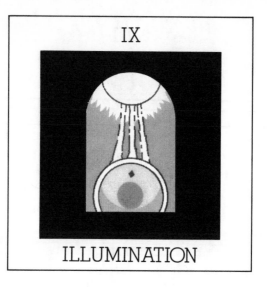

IX

ILLUMINATION

IX. HOUSE OF THE ILLUMINATION
"I REALIZE"

This area is concerned with the search for what is really true, for the basic principles in life, for what one truly believes in and values.

The energies (Stars) of The Illumination are those of "The Prayer" and "The Watcher." The condition (State) is that of Snow. The expressions (Star-crosses) are those of the Knight and the Ladder. The Gift is the Wing, and realization (Key) is through the Mask. Significant attitudes (Gates) are symbolized by the Rod and the Cherry. Fulfillment (Sign) is the Coffin.

The Seas of Pyramids and Labyrinths (VIII and IX) surround this Garden of "I REALIZE."

PERFECT FORM

X. HOUSE OF THE PERFECT FORM
"I PERFECT"

This area has to do with dealing with the truth, with confronting limitations and dealing with authority — both with others and within oneself.

The energies (Stars) of The Perfect Form are those of "The Watcher" and "The Deliverer." The condition (State) is that of Fog. The expressions (Star-crosses) are those of the Swan and the Window. The Gift is the Tongue, and realization (Key) is through the Block. Significant attitudes (Gates) are symbolized by the Cherry and the Arrow. Fulfillment (Sign) is the Field.

The Seas of Labyrinths and Quiet Flowers (IX and X) surround this Garden of "I PERFECT."

XI

UNIFICATION

XI. HOUSE OF THE UNIFICATION

"I EXPAND"

The emphasis here is on one's highest hopes, to surpass limitation and reach for freedom — not just for oneself but for all.

The energies (Stars) of The Unification are those of "The Deliverer" and "The Seeker." The condition (State) is that of Air. The expressions (Star-crosses) are those of the Sun and the Fountain. The Gift is the Morning, and realization (Key) is through the Wand. Significant attitudes (Gates) are symbolized by the Arrow and the Siphon. Fulfillment (Sign) is the Crown.

The Seas of Quiet Flowers and Stars Within (X and XI) surround this Garden of "I EXPAND."

XII

DISSOLUTION

XII. HOUSE OF THE DISSOLUTION
"I MERGE"

This area represents achieving fulfillment, and through absolute completion, transcending and dissolving back into the Whole.

The energies (Stars) of The Dissolution are those of "The Seeker" and "The Dreamer." The condition (State) is that of the Pool. The expressions (Star-crosses) are those of the Monk and the Candle. The Gift is the Rope, and realization (Key) is through the Ring. Significant attitudes (Gates) are symbolized by the Siphon and the Tower. Fulfillment (Sign) is the Key.

The Seas of Stars Within and Dreams (XI and XII) surround this Garden of "I MERGE."

The Twelve Seas

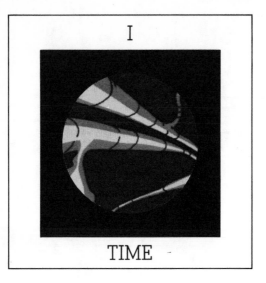

I

TIME

I. SEA OF TIME
EXPERIENCING

In this Sea, we exist and experience. Duration leads to sequence, and we separate then from now, this from that, and you from me. Everybody wants to do something; we stir.

Here shines the Star of Impulse, "The Doer." He fills this place with the desire to experience. The expressions (Star-crosses) are the Wanderer and the Lover. The realizations (Keys) are in the Cup and the Rose. The way in and out is through the Gate of the Glove, where PROJECTING IDENTITIES gains access and ACCEPTING ASSISTANCE creates an exit.

The Sea of Time is shared between the first and second Houses, The First Cause and The Matrix.

II

INNOCENCE

II. SEA OF INNOCENCE
GROWING

In this place, we still hear the voice of "The Speaker," that which sent us forth and which beckons us onward. Under the Star of Reaching, we GROW and pursue living.

The expressions (Star-crosses) are the Child and the Tree. The realizations (Keys) are through the Rose and the Powder. Access and exit are through the Gate of the Ice, where CLARITY gets one in and CHANGEABILITY lets one out. Here, we recall our inner guidance.

The Sea of Innocence is shared between the second and third Houses, The Matrix and The Motion.

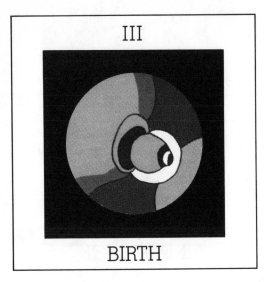

III

BIRTH

III. SEA OF BIRTH
ADJUSTING

In this Sea, the Star of Change brings forth new things. "The Mover" acts; the energy of ADJUSTING makes way for new emergence. This is the East, where dawn brings opportunity.

The expressions (Star-crosses) are the Egg and the Chest. The realizations (Keys) are in the Powder and the Serpent. The Gate is the Stone, providing entry through INTEGRITY and exit through STEADFASTNESS.

The Sea of Birth is shared between the third and fourth Houses, The Motion and The Pure Water.

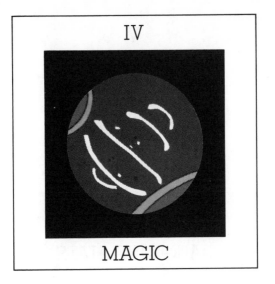

IV

MAGIC

IV. SEA OF MAGIC

INTERNALIZING

Here, the Mystery comes forth, just beneath the fabric of life, a bouyant undercoat woven by "The Feeler." Through the energy of INTERNALIZING, that which is latent congeals. We are not powerless and simply placed on Earth; we feel the wonder within.

The expressions (Star-crosses) are the Moon and the Glass. The realizations (Keys) are in the Serpent and the Chain. The Gate of the Hole provides access through PERCEPTION OF OTHER REALITIES and exit through OPENNESS.

The Sea of Magic is shared between the fourth and fifth Houses, The Pure Water and The Spirit Incarnate.

V

LAUGHING HATS

V. SEA OF LAUGHING HATS

EXTERNALIZING

In this Sea are all life's actors, each with permission to act out his or her role. "The Player" eggs us on. He encourages us to enjoy being onstage with his energy of EXTERNALIZING. We can be anything we choose, at least for a moment.

The expressions (Star-crosses) are the Jester and the Duck. The realizations (Keys) are through the Chain and the Robe. Entry and exit are through the Gate of the Sword, where SELF-EXPRESSION makes a way in and DISCRIMINATING creates the way out.

The Sea of Laughing Hats is shared between the fifth and sixth Houses, The Spirit Incarnate and The Grand Plan.

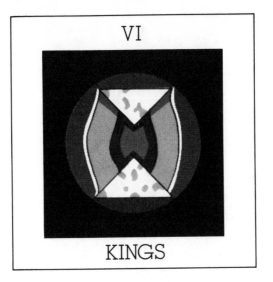

VI

KINGS

VI. SEA OF KINGS
INTEGRATING

In the Southerly position, "Majesty," the Star of Bowing, reigns. The energy of INTEGRATING calls forth our best, seeking a blend of inner and outer urges and exposure of our transcendent nature. We glimpse our personal glory and our collective heritage.

The expressions (Star-crosses) are the Leaf and the Maiden. The realizations (Keys) are through the Robe and the Gate. The Gate to Kings is through the Token, where entry comes from APPRECIATING OTHERS and exit from EXPRESSING INTENT.

The Sea of Kings is shared between the sixth and seventh Houses, The Grand Plan and The Perfect Union.

VII

MUSIC

VII. SEA OF MUSIC
WEIGHING

In this place, we experience "The Dancer," the vibration of life between polarities. We feel the pulsating current of existence and know the balance of things through the energy of WEIGHING.

The expressions (Star-crosses) are the Bell and the Butterfly. The realizations (Keys) are in the Gate and the Wind. Entry and exit are provided by the Gate of the Handle, a paradoxical mix of INITIATIVE and RESPONSIBILITY.

The Sea of Music is shared between the seventh and eighth Houses, The Perfect Union and The Power.

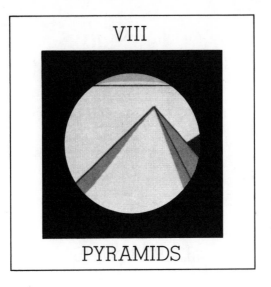

VIII

PYRAMIDS

VIII. SEA OF PYRAMIDS
TRUSTING

In this Sea, we discover the heights to which we can aspire and, equally, the depths to which we can tumble. Here, the Star of Hope shines ardently; "The Prayer" communes most sincerely. But his cause is serious and deep; self righteousness is a temptation. One must examine the motives for great deeds, or fall.

The expressions (Star-crosses) are the Knight and the Knife. The realizations (Keys) are in the Wind and the Mask. The Gate to Pyramids is through the Rod, where COMMAND provides entry and DISCRETION makes an exit.

The Sea of Pyramids is shared between the eighth and ninth Houses, The Power and The Illumination.

IX

LABYRINTHS

IX. SEA OF LABYRINTHS

PERCEIVING

In this place, we view the complexities of life along with the seem-ing ultimate arbitrariness of it all. This is the West, where the Star of Austerity perplexes us with the steady gaze of "The Watcher." The energy of PERCEIVING is intense, unblinking. It is the puzzle of puzzles, the challenge of silence, the unuttered question with no conceivable answer. It is the place of the most final of questions.

The expressions (Star-crosses) are the Swan and the Ladder. The realizations (Keys) are in the Mask and the Block. The Gate is the Cherry, where GETTING INVOLVED creates access and INNER COMPLETION makes the way out.

The Sea of Labyrinths is shared between the ninth and tenth Houses, The Illumination and The Perfect Form.

X

QUIET FLOWERS

X. SEA OF QUIET FLOWERS
FREEING

Over this Sea shines the Star of Independence. The light of "The Deliverer" urges us to set our selves free. Together we create a field of beauty with its own reason and purpose. Free yet together — that is this place.

The expressions (Star-crosses) are the Sun and the Window. The realizations (Keys) are in the Block and the Wand. The Gate is the Arrow, where SPONTANEITY creates a way in and DECISIVENESS makes the way out.

The Sea of Quiet Flowers is shared between the tenth and eleventh Houses, The Perfect Form and The Unification.

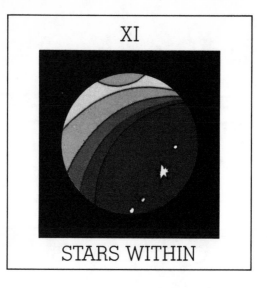

XI

STARS WITHIN

XI. SEA OF STARS WITHIN

DISCOVERING

Here, we experience our own transcendence. The Star of Aspiration shines, and "The Seeker" is revealed to himself through the transparent energy of DISCOVERING. We find we are god-stuff and star-stuff. We see through ourselves to the truth; we were never apart. We become both mind and energy, Star and Gate as one.

The expressions (Star-crosses) are the Monk and the Fountain. The realizations (Keys) are in the Wand and the Ring. The Gate is the Siphon, where EXCHANGE is the way in and RELEASE is the way out.

The Sea of Stars Within is shared between the eleventh and twelfth Houses, The Unification and The Dissolution.

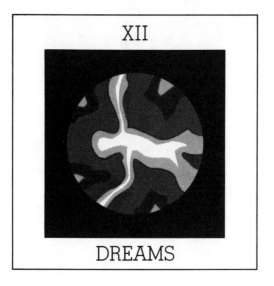

XII

DREAMS

XII. SEA OF DREAMS
IMAGINING

In this place, one experiences the beginning and ending of things — the spark, the idea. It is the North, the unknowable, the Mystery. It is where all things come from, the unlimited potential of "The Dreamer." We swirl in all that can be, before and after it is real.

The expressions (Star-crosses) are the Magician and the Candle. The realizations (Keys) are in the Ring and the Cup. The Gate is the Tower, where REFLECTION provides access and FOCUSING ATTENTION makes a way out.

The Sea of Dreams is shared between the twelfth and first Houses, The Dissolution and The First Cause.

The Ninety-Six
Symbolic Cards

LIST OF SYMBOLIC CARDS

STARS (A–L)

A. Star of Impulse
B. Star of Reaching
C. Star of Change
D. Star of Inwardness
E. Star of Laugh
F. Star of Bowing
G. Star of Indecision
H. Star of Hope
I. Star of Austerity
J. Star of Independence
K. Star of Aspiration
L. Star of Patience

STATES (1–12)

1. Sand
2. Lightning
3. Rain
4. Mud
5. Fire
6. Water
7. Earth
8. Thunder
9. Snow
10. Fog
11. Air
12. Pool

STAR-CROSSES (13–36)

13. Magician
14. Lover
15. Child
16. Egg
17. Moon
18. Jester
19. Maiden
20. Butterfly
21. Knight
22. Swan
23. Sun
24. Monk
25. Wanderer
26. Tree
27. Chest
28. Glass
29. Duck
30. Leaf
31. Bell
32. Knife
33. Ladder
34. Window
35. Fountain
36. Candle

LIST OF SYMBOLIC CARDS *(Cont.)*

GIFTS (37–48)

37. Root
38. Eye
39. Tunnel
40. Harp
41. Circle
42. Chair
43. Letter
44. Wheel
45. Wing
46. Tongue
47. Morning
48. Rope

KEYS (49–60)

49. Cup
50. Rose
51. Powder
52. Serpent
53. Chain
54. Robe
55. Gate
56. Wind
57. Mask
58. Block
59. Wand
60. Ring

GATES (61–72)

61. Tower
62. Glove
63. Ice
64. Stone
65. Hole
66. Sword
67. Token
68. Handle
69. Rod
70. Cherry
71. Arrow
72. Siphon

SIGNS (73–84)

73. Mountain
74. Cake
75. Cross
76. Sea
77. Star
78. Lamp
79. Cave
80. Pearl
81. Coffin
82. Field
83. Crown
84. Key

THE STAR CARDS — ENERGIES
A through L

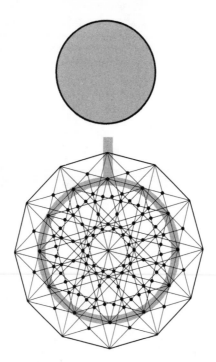

The Stars represent Consciousness in Energy. These are archetypal aspects of all beingness so pervasive in living that only such terms as light, energy or moods can describe them and their effects in our lives. They are profound yet elusive qualities, ranging from noticeable outbursts of activity to energies so passive they seem not to be present.

The ring of Stars is the outermost labeled points on the Circle Pattern, shown in bright yellow. Within their ring lie all the other named points on the Circle (1-84). In great part, it is the intermingling of the Star energies which creates the particular symbols at the other intersections. Their web of light symbolizes the very fabric of our existence.

Each Star card carries the name of an imaginary being on the card's word side. This being typifies the kind of energy involved. A bold-faced word below the name also describes the kind of mood or atmosphere the card symbolizes.

Each Star is situated in such a way on the Circle that it is shared between two Houses. Its energy plays an integral part in expressing the qualities of its Houses. Each Star is also over a Sea area and, again, is essential in describing a particular Sea.

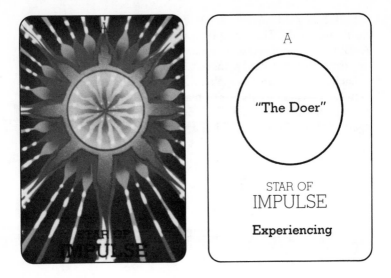

A. The Star of IMPULSE

This Star's energy is all about do anything, be anything, try anything. It is typified by "The Doer," a being who does, and does, and does. The energy is that of EXPERIENCING, regardless of purpose, regardless of outcome, regardless.

The Star of Impulse is shared between the first and second Houses. Therefore, the energy of "The Doer" is part of "I AM" and "I WANT." It also creates the light of the Sea of Time (I).

On the picture side of this card, the Star's center shows energy streaming out in all directions from a central point.

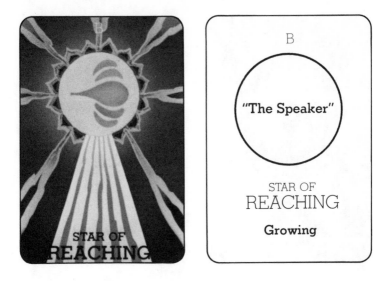

B. The Star of REACHING

The Star of Reaching is about energy channeled in a specific direction, reaching for something. Behind this is the energy of "The Speaker," the being who encourages us to go and increase. The energy is that of GROWING, multiplying who we are and what we have. The Speaker is the timeless impetus to go beyond limitation.

The Star of Reaching is shared between the second and third Houses. Therefore the energy of "The Speaker" is part of "I WANT" and "I RELATE." It also creates the light of the Sea of Innocence (II).

On the picture side of the card, the Star's center shows energy moving in a specific direction; the light from the Star is similarly channeled.

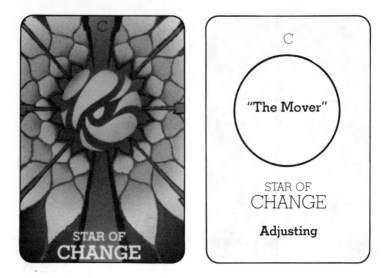

C. The Star of CHANGE

The Star of Change is about redirecting energy, the atmosphere of changing course. This is typified by "The Mover" who brings change by his very presence and through his every act. The energy is that of ADJUSTING, making way for change and progress.

The Star of Change is shared between the third and fourth Houses. Therefore, the energy of "The Mover" is part of "I RELATE" and "I FEEL." It also creates the light of the Sea of Birth (III).

On the picture side of the card, the Star's center shows energy moving at right angles to itself, denoting a change in direction.

D. The Star of INWARDNESS

The Star of Inwardness is about the energy experienced within oneself. It is typified by "The Feeler," the being who feels outside events on the inside. This is the energy of INTERNALIZING, of knowing one's emotions and inner drives, of taking things to heart.

The Star of Inwardness is shared between the fourth and fifth Houses. Therefore, the energy of "The Feeler" is part of "I FEEL" and "I PROJECT." It also creates the light of the Sea of Magic (IV).

On the picture side of the card, the Star's center shows a spiraling inward, creating a subdued outer light.

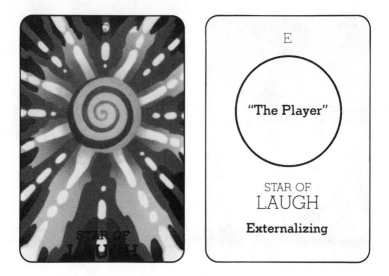

E. The Star of LAUGH

The Star of Laugh describes exhuberant, expressive energy, typified by the idea of "The Player" who can act out any role called for. This is the energy of EXTERNALIZING, vitality made visible.

The Star of Laugh is shared between the fifth and sixth Houses. Therefore, "The Player" is part of "I PROJECT" and "I BECOME." It also creates the light of the Sea of Laughing Hats (V).

On the picture side of the card, the Star's center shows energy spiraling outward, surrounded by bright, dancing light.

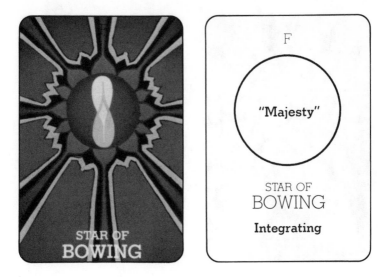

F. The Star of BOWING

The Star of Bowing combines the previous two Stars (D and E), acknowledging the value of each, blending in- and out-flowing into the energy of INTEGRATING. This is typified by the term "Majesty," the regal harmonizing of flow. It is that to which we bow in ourselves and in others.

The Star of Bowing is shared between the sixth and seventh Houses. Therefore, the energy of "Majesty" is part of "I BECOME" and "I INTERACT." It also creates the light of the Sea of Kings (VI).

On the picture side of the card, the Star's center shows energies moving in opposing directions, flowing through one another in balance, against a majestic light.

G. The Star of INDECISION

The Star of Indecision describes the dance of energy that occurs between polarities. This vibration essential to all life is epitomized by "The Dancer," animated by dualities, creating a cosmic dance while WEIGHING the difference between two poles.

The Star of Indecision is shared between the seventh and eighth Houses. Therefore, the energy of "The Dancer" is part of "I INTERACT" and "I CARE." It also creates the light of the Sea of Music (VII).

On the picture side of the card, the Star's center shows energy swimming in two directions and a vibrating light issuing from the Star.

H. The Star of HOPE

The Star of Hope is a passive energy, epitomized by "The Prayer," a being who waits for action to come from outside itself. The energy is TRUSTING, a faith in a higher or wiser source, a surrender of will.

The Star of Hope is shared between the eighth and ninth Houses. Therefore, the energy of "The Prayer" is part of "I CARE" and "I REALIZE." It also creates the light of the Sea of Pyramids (VIII).

On the picture side of the card, the Star's center is shown as receptive, expecting energy from outside itself; yet it emits a steady, secure radiance.

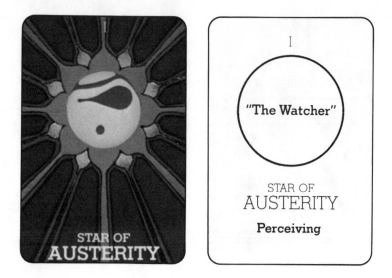

I. The Star of AUSTERITY

The Star of Austerity denotes a cold, clear look. It is typified by "The Watcher," a being whose only task is to truly see. The energy is that of PERCEIVING, of finding what is really there and what is really going on.

The Star of Austerity is shared between the ninth and tenth Houses. Therefore, "The Watcher" is part of "I REALIZE" and "I PERFECT." It also creates the light of the Sea of Labyrinths (IX).

On the picture side of the card, the Star's center shows energy separated from a dot, or consciousness separating itself from an object, in order to truly perceive it.

J. The Star of INDEPENDENCE

The Star of Independence is about non-attachment, to things or to people. It is typified by "The Deliverer," the being who releases ties and bonds. The energy is FREEING, loosening, making space.

The Star of Independence is shared between the tenth and eleventh Houses. Therefore, the energy of "The Deliverer" is part of "I PERFECT" and "I EXPAND." It also creates the light of the Sea of Quiet Flowers (X).

On the picture side of the card, the Star's center shows energy moving away from a point, or consciousness removing itself from something.

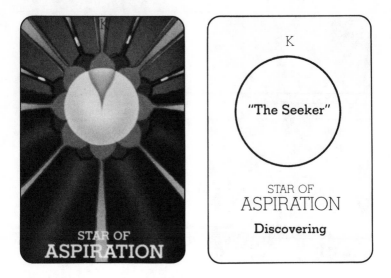

STAR OF
ASPIRATION

K
"The Seeker"

STAR OF
ASPIRATION

Discovering

K. The Star of ASPIRATION

The Star of Aspiration is about transcendence. Typifying this is "The Seeker," the being who is always looking forward and looking beyond. The energy is that of DISCOVERING; the more you look, the more you find. It is not a matter of surpassing others but of transcending one's own views.

The Star of Aspiration is shared between the eleventh and twelfth Houses. Therefore, the energy of "The Seeker" is part of "I EXPAND" and "I MERGE." It also creates the light of the Sea of Stars Within (XI).

On the picture side of the card, the Star's center shows energy, or consciousness, rising up and out of its own light.

L. The Star of PATIENCE

The Star of Patience is the energy of ideas, or the idea of having energy. Typifying this is "The Dreamer," the being who dreams of the possibilities and potentials of all that could be. The energy is that of IMAGINING, to dream the dream, to sprout the idea.

The Star of Patience is shared between the twelfth and first Houses. Therefore, the energy of "The Dreamer" is part of "I MERGE" and "I AM." It also creates the light of the Sea of Dreams (XII).

On the picture side of the card, the Star's center shows swirling activity, much going on but undefined, radiating a quiet but dynamic light.

THE STATE CARDS — CONDITIONS
1 through 12

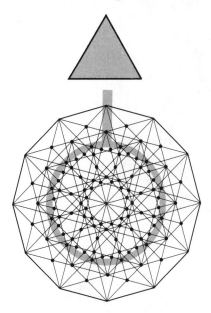

The State Cards are Aspects of Form. They symbolize outer states, conditions and environments that can be present in various situations. Like the world of form, these conditions can be both beneficial and detrimental, depending on how we perceive them and deal with them. The word side of each State card lists both the advantages and disadvantages that can be involved with a particular symbol.

On the Circle Pattern, the ring of State points lies just within the ring of the Stars. There is one State point at the top of each Garden area in each House; it describes the inherent condition that goes with the House.

Each State point has two Stars next to it on the Circle Pattern. The energies of these two Stars mix together to create the particular State. These energies lock together, in a sense, creating a form or condition, much in the same way positive protons and negative electrons attract and revolve around each other in the structure of the atom, the basic building block of the material world.

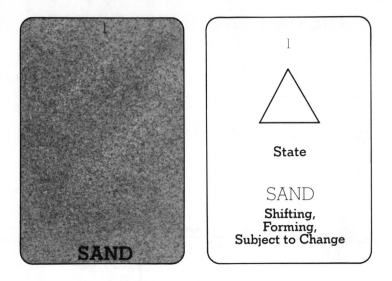

1. The SAND

The Sand symbolizes the subtle condition of readiness, a kind of SHIFTING, like looking for footing. It is also FORMING, taking shape, making forms out of itself. The Sand, though, is moved by other elements, so its forms are SUBJECT TO CHANGE, rearrangement, even to being scattered.

The Sand is in the House of The First Cause (I), and it represents a mixing of the Stars of Patience and Impulse. Therefore, the Sand is the condition of "I AM," an outgrowth of the energy of IMAGINING combining with EXPERIENCING.

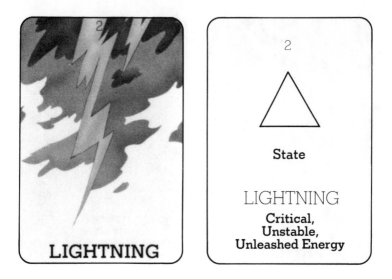

2. The LIGHTNING

The Lightning is a condition that is CRITICAL, one that seems to border on chaos, yet is loaded with energy. It is a condition that is UNSTABLE; something is bound to happen, but no one knows where the lightning will strike. It is a state in which great amounts of ENERGY are UNLEASHED. What may have been static before is now undeniably dynamic and powerful.

The Lightning is in the House of The Matrix (II), and it represents a mixing of the Stars of Impulse and Reaching. Therefore, the Lightning is the condition of "I WANT," an outgrowth of the energy of EXPERIENCING combining with GROWING.

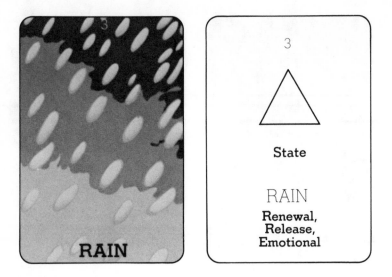

RAIN

3

State

RAIN

Renewal,
Release,
Emotional

3. The RAIN

The Rain is a condition that washes away the old; it brings RENEWAL, a break followed by a fresh beginning. It prompts RELEASE, a freeing, a loosening up. It is also an EMOTIONAL condition, where feelings find expression.

The Rain is in the House of The Motion (III), and it represents the mixing of the Stars of Reaching and Change. Therefore, the Rain symbolizes the condition of "I RELATE," an outgrowth of the energy of GROWING combining with ADJUSTING.

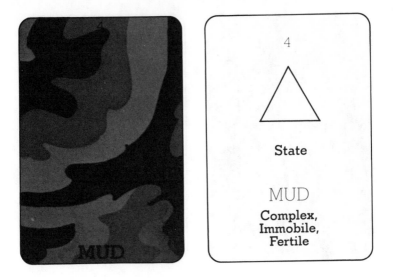

4. The MUD

The Mud is a state where things seem to come to a halt. It symbolizes a COMPLEX condition, with much to consider. It is more or less static, IMMOBILE, not going anywhere. It is also a FERTILE state, a condition that nurtures new growth or re-evaluation.

The Mud is in the House of The Pure Water (IV), and it represents the mixing of the Stars of Change and Inwardness. Therefore, the Mud is the condition of "I FEEL," an outgrowth of the energy of ADJUSTING combining with INTERNALIZING.

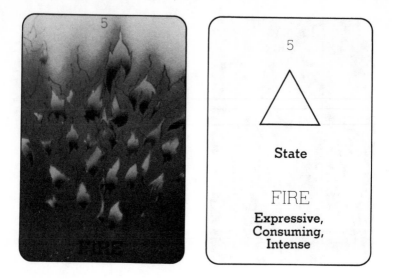

5. The FIRE

The Fire symbolizes a volatile condition. It is at once EXPRESSIVE and outgoing yet CONSUMING, exacting its toll. It is an INTENSE state, whether it reflects the heat of battle or that of passion.

The Fire is in the House of The Spirit Incarnate (V), and it represents the mixing of the Stars of Inwardness and Laugh. Therefore, the Fire is the condition of "I PROJECT," an outgrowth of the energy of INTERNALIZING combining with EXTERNALIZING.

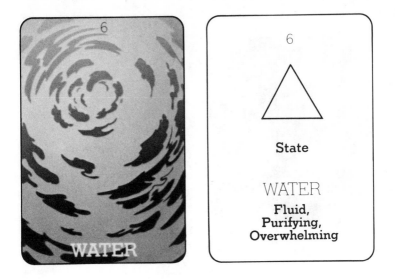

6. The WATER

The Water is a state that is FLUID, bending, being open and receptive. Its condition is one of PURIFYING, cleansing old wounds. The Water can also be OVERWHELMING, a condition in which one could drown or be swept away.

The Water is in the House of The Grand Plan (VI), and it represents the mixing of the Stars of Laugh and Bowing. The Water symbolizes the condition of "I BECOME," an outgrowth of the energy of EXTERNALIZING combining with INTEGRATING.

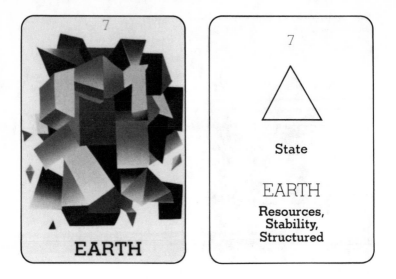

EARTH

7. The EARTH

The Earth as a condition symbolizes RESOURCES, the wealth of ingredients and possibilities at our fingertips. It is also a state of STABILITY, of being on firm ground. And it represents conditions that are STRUCTURED. Roles and ground rules are made apparent.

The Earth is in the House of The Perfect Union (VII), and it represents the mixing of the Stars of Bowing and Indecision. Therefore, the Earth symbolizes the condition of "I INTERACT," an outgrowth of the energy of INTEGRATING combining with WEIGHING.

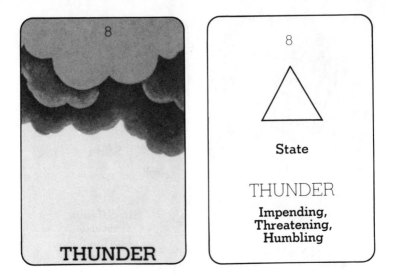

8. The THUNDER

Distant thunder alerts us to a storm, and so the Thunder is an IMPENDING state — something is about to happen, probably something out of our control. It can be a THREATENING condition. What will happen? Will anything be destroyed? The questions hang in the air . . . waiting. The Thunder is also a HUMBLING condition. We realize our own smallness in the face of the bigness of the moving universe.

The Thunder is in the House of The Power (VIII), and it represents the mixing of the Stars of Indecision and Hope. Therefore, the Thunder is the condition of "I CARE," an outgrowth of the energy of WEIGHING combining with TRUSTING.

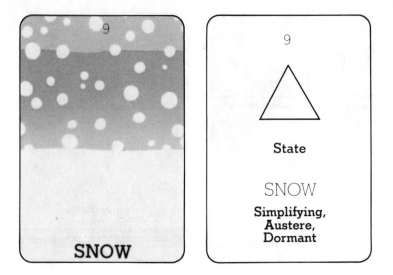

SNOW

State

SNOW

Simplifying,
Austere,
Dormant

9. The SNOW

A snow cover softens the landscape in a SIMPLIFYING gesture. It is a condition as stark as it is beautiful; things are reduced to black and white. The Snow is an AUSTERE state, cold yet clear. Under the Snow, conditions are DORMANT; life is frozen or hibernating waiting for the new season to come.

The Snow is in the House of The Illumination (IX), and it represents the mixing of the Stars of Hope and Austerity. The Snow is the condition of "I REALIZE," an outgrowth of the energy of TRUSTING combining with PERCEIVING.

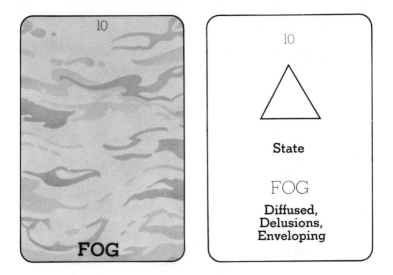

10. The FOG

The Fog is a DIFFUSED condition, one in which borders are unclear, steering is difficult. It is a state of DELUSIONS; distance is lost, nothing is as normal, and everything is confusing. It is ENVELOPING. Once surrounded by fog, one feels lost in it and ruled by it.

The Fog is in the House of The Perfect Form (X), and it represents the mixing of The Stars of Austerity and Independence. Therefore, the Fog is the condition of "I PERFECT," an outgrowth of the energy of PERCEIVING combining with FREEING.

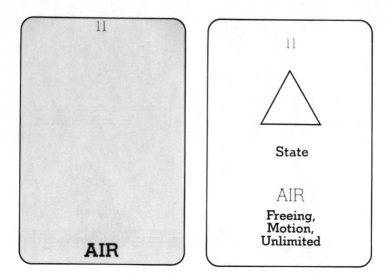

11. The AIR

The Air is a FREEING condition, one unfettered by difficulties. It is a state of MOTION, free movement and intermingling. It is also UNLIMITED; the air sweeps the entire landscape without straining against other forces.

The Air is in the House of the Unification (XI), and it represents the mixing of the Stars of Independence and Aspiration. Therefore, the Air is the condition of "I EXPAND," an outgrowth of the energy of FREEING combining with DISCOVERING.

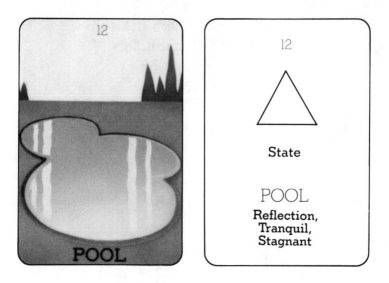

12. The POOL

The Pool is a state of repose, a condition of REFLECTION and evaluation, a rest. It is a TRANQUIL state, without tension or stress. Yet it can be a STAGNANT condition of resting on one's laurels or being afraid to go forward.

The Pool is in the House of the Dissolution (XII), and it represents the mixing of the Stars of Aspiration and Patience. Therefore, the Pool is the condition of "I MERGE," an outgrowth of the energy of DISCOVERING combining with IMAGINING.

THE STAR-CROSS CARDS
SELF-EXPRESSIONS
13 through 36

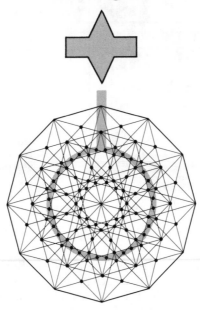

The Star-cross cards are Aspects of Self-expression, ways for showing ourselves to the world. Each card describes a character, a side of oneself, that may be at play in a particular situation. Each character has several words associated with it. Each shows a way that the character might be seen, depending on the viewpoint. For example, The Lover can be a giving and intimate role, but it could be perceived by another as being possessive and demanding. Each Star-cross shows the pluses and minuses of ways we can express ourselves.

On the Circle Pattern, the Star-crosses are the double ring of 24 orange-colored points. There are two Star-cross points in each House, on either side of the upper portion of the Garden area. There are also two of these types of points near the top of each Sea area. Each Star-cross symbol is an expression of the qualities of both the House and Sea it is in.

The Star-cross points are the only points on the Circle Pattern that have unequal amounts of Star energies, as seen by the unequal lengths of the four yellow lines from a Star-cross to the Stars connected to it. The Star closest to the Star-cross point is the strongest ingredient in the symbol. The next closest Star is a strong but secondary ingredient, and the third and fourth are weaker influences by comparison. The text on the cards notes the two strongest energies for each Star-cross, listed in order of closeness to the point. It is the imbalance of energies that gives the Star-crosses, aspects of self-expression, their unique character among the STAR+GATE symbols.

13. The MAGICIAN

The Magician is about that part of us that is ADEPT, knowing the world and how to work with the forces in it. As such, the Magician is a TRANSFORMER, able to bring about change, sometimes surprisingly. The Magician knows how to use his knowledge to his own ends and can be seen as a MANIPULATOR. In all, the Magician performs feats that few others can, and almost anyone would regard him as INGENIOUS.

The Magician is composed primarily of the Stars of Patience and Impulse, and it lies in the House of The First Cause (I). Therefore it is expressing "I AM" through the energies of IMAGINING and EXPERIENCING. It is also an expression of the Sea of Dreams (XII).

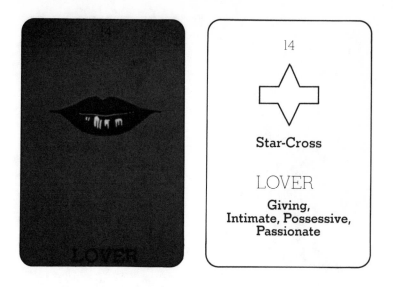

14. The LOVER

The Lover is about the GIVING side of ourselves, an outflowing but INTIMATE side. At times the giving can become demanding; the Lover becomes POSSESSIVE and will not let the recipient go; it wants to cling. The Lover's pursuits are PASSIONATE, laced with zeal and a certain determination.

The Lover is composed principally of the Stars of Impulse and Reaching, and it lies in the House of The Matrix (II). Therefore, the Lover is expressing "I WANT" through the energies of EXPERIENCING and GROWING. It is also an expression of the Sea of Time (I).

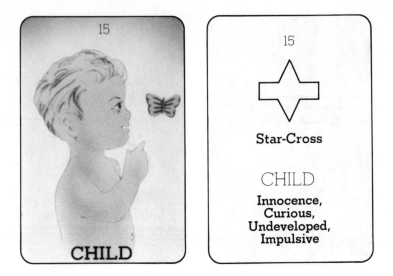

CHILD

15
Star-Cross

CHILD

Innocence,
Curious,
Undeveloped,
Impulsive

15. The CHILD

The Child symbolizes the part of us that is new and open — our INNOCENCE. The Child is curious; everything waits to be explored. It is also UNDEVELOPED, not fully grown or mature. And by nature, the Child is IMPULSIVE in its desires. What it wants comes first, regardless of what else is occurring.

The Child is composed principally of the Stars of Reaching and Change, and it lies in the Garden of the House of The Motion (III). The Child, therefore, is expressing "I RELATE" through the energies of GROWING and ADJUSTING. It is also an expression the Sea of Innocence (II).

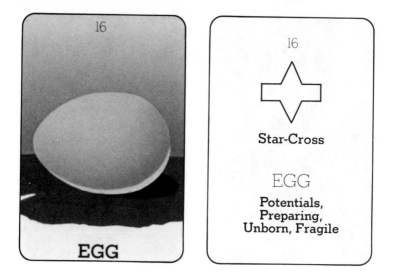

16. The EGG

The Egg describes the latent part of ourselves, the yet-to-be. It symbolizes POTENTIALS, expressing what we could become. It is what we are PREPARING in ourselves that is noticed by others — something that is as yet UNBORN. It is also FRAGILE in this condition; rough handling could change its fate.

The Egg is composed primarily of the Stars of Change and Inwardness, and it lies in the House of The Pure Water (IV). Therefore, the Egg is expressing "I FEEL" through the energies of ADJUSTING and INTERNALIZING. It is also an expression of the Sea of Birth (III).

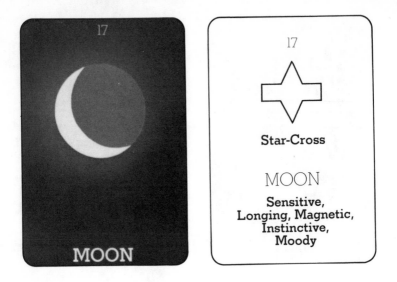

17. The MOON

The Moon is about our SENSITIVE side, one that is quiet and sometimes hard to read. It expresses a LONGING that is often undefined. It is MAGNETIC; others are drawn to it. Actions seem INSTINCTIVE, unexplainable but following nature. The Moon is also perceived as MOODY, emotional.

The Moon is composed principally of the Stars of Inwardness and Laugh, and it lies in the House of The Spirit Incarnate (V). Therefore, the Moon is expressing "I PROJECT" through the energies of INTERNALIZING and EXTERNALIZING, with an emphasis on the former. It is also an expression of the Sea of Magic (IV).

Star-Cross

JESTER

Humor, Expressive, Mimicking, Candid, Undignified

18. The JESTER

Our lighter (and equally truthful) side is symbolized by the Jester. He has HUMOR; he is funny. He is EXPRESSIVE of what he thinks and sees. Often the Jester is MIMICKING the ways and roles of others. He is almost always CANDID in his appraisal of situations. The Jester can also be UNDIGNIFIED, untactful.

The Jester is composed primarily of the Stars of Laugh and Bowing, and it lies in the House of The Grand Plan (VI). The Jester's role is expressing "I BECOME" through the energies of EXTERNALIZING and INTEGRATING. It is also an expression of the Sea of Laughing Hats (V).

19. The MAIDEN

Symbolizing our vision of PURITY and BEAUTY is the Maiden, the side of us that seeks the best for everyone. There is a GENTLE exterior. It is VIRGIN in that it is uncompromised and undebatable. And it is a side that can seem VULNERABLE to outside influences and to the wills of others.

The Maiden is composed principally of the Stars of Bowing and Indecision, and it lies in the House of the Perfect Union (VII). Therefore, the Maiden is expressing "I INTERACT" through the energies of INTEGRATING and WEIGHING. It is also an expression of the Sea of Kings (VI).

20. The BUTTERFLY

The Butterfly is about the rather experimental side of ourselves, by which we attempt to act in new ways or transform old ones. It can appear ELUSIVE, something that is hard to get hold of. It is DELICATE as any new thing is. It is EMERGING, coming out in plain sight. The Butterfly is something CAREFREE, beyond limitation, and even FICKLE in its quest for new associations.

The Butterfly is composed primarily of the Stars of Indecision and Hope, and it lies in the House of The Power (VIII). Therefore, the Butterfly is expressing "I CARE" through the energies of WEIGHING and TRUSTING. It is also an expression of the Sea of Music (VII).

Star-Cross

KNIGHT

Courageous, Loyal, Adventurous, Idealistic, Opportunistic

21. The KNIGHT

The Knight symbolizes the noble side of ourselves, that which is COURAGEOUS in its endeavors and LOYAL to its cause. The Knight is ADVENTUROUS and seeks new territories and kingdoms. It is IDEALISTIC, measuring others against lofty standards. At times, the Knight is OPPORTUNISTIC, seeking personal gratification in the name of a great cause.

The Knight is composed principally of the Stars of Hope and Austerity, and it lies in the House of The Illumination (IX). Therefore, the Knight is expressing "I REALIZE" through the energies of TRUSTING and PERCEIVING. It is also an expression of the Sea of Pyramids (VIII).

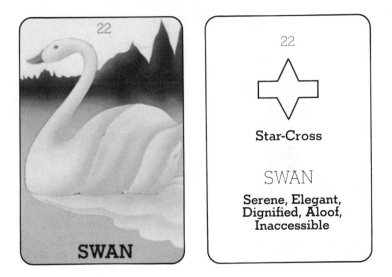

22. The SWAN

The Swan is about our calm and together side. This is where one looks or feels SERENE, comfortable within. It is ELEGANT even if simple, and DIGNIFIED regardless of custom. Yet the facade can appear ALOOF, above the rest of the world and its troubles, or even INACCESSIBLE, driving away the interest of others.

The Swan is composed primarily of the Stars of Austerity and Independence, and it lies in the House of The Perfect Form (X). The Swan's role is expressing "I PERFECT" through the energies of PERCEIVING and FREEING. It is also an expression of the Sea of Labyrinths (IX).

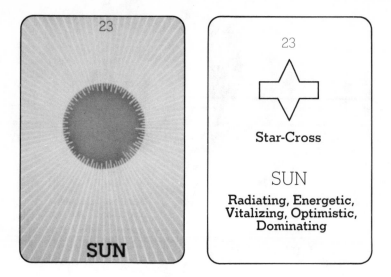

23. The SUN

The Sun is the expansive and warm side of ourselves. It is RADIATING itself to the rest of the world. It feels ENERGETIC and is VITALIZING to those around it. As the "sunny side," it is the expression of OPTIMISM. Yet as a strong, outflowing force it can also be a DOMINATING influence, seeking to have its way be *the* way.

The Sun is composed principally of the Stars of Independence and Aspiration, and it lies in the House of The Unification (XI). Therefore, the Sun is expressing "I EXPAND" through the energies of FREEING and DISCOVERING. It is also an expression of the Sea of Quiet Flowers (X).

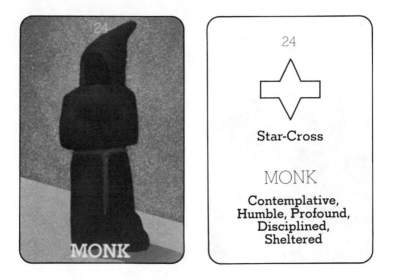

24. The MONK

The Monk is about the philosophical and thoughtful side of ourselves. The Monk is CONTEMPLATIVE, pondering the nature and essence of things. In this pursuit he is HUMBLE and often exhibits a DISCIPLINED life style. His inner journey leads to actions or words that are PROFOUND and far-reaching in their impact. Some will view him, though, as SHELTERED from the everyday world.

The Monk is composed primarily of the Stars of Aspiration and Patience, and it lies in the House of The Dissolution (XII). The Monk, therefore, is expressing "I MERGE" through the energies of DISCOVERING and IMAGINING. It is also an expression of the Sea of Stars Within (XI).

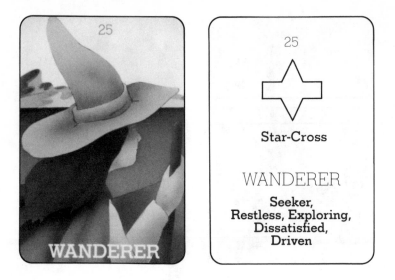

25. The WANDERER

The Wanderer represents our searching side, that of the SEEKER looking for meaning, for purpose. It is a RESTLESS aspect, one that is constantly EXPLORING what the world has to offer. It is DISSATISFIED with the everyday and commonplace. The Wanderer is DRIVEN to satisfy an inner craving for answers.

The Wanderer is composed principally of the Stars of Impulse and Patience, and it lies in the Garden of the House of The First Cause (I). Therefore, the Wanderer is expressing "I AM" through the energies of EXPERIENCING and IMAGINING. It is also an expression of the Sea of Time (I).

26. The TREE

The Tree describes the mature side of our nature, the part that is DEVELOPED, grown-up. It is also a catalog of KNOWLEDGE built up over time. It reflects STABILITY, having withstood the test of time. It also describes a rather TRADITIONAL outlook, having seen many things come and go. And the Tree, too, can be SHELTERING to others, a place where rest can be sought in the midst of a storm.

The Tree is composed primarily of the Stars of Reaching and Impulse, and it lies in the House of The Matrix (II). The Tree, therefore, is expressing "I WANT" through GROWING and EXPERIENCING. It is also an expression of the Sea of Innocence (II).

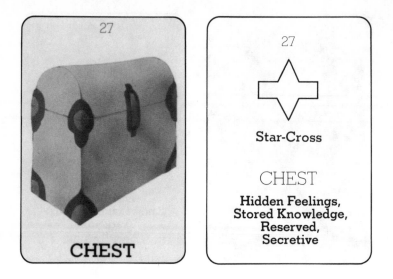

Star-Cross

CHEST

Hidden Feelings,
Stored Knowledge,
Reserved,
Secretive

CHEST

27. The CHEST

The Chest is about our reserved side, what is held back from the world. It symbolizes HIDDEN FEELINGS, emotions that are held in check for one reason or another. The Chest can also contain STORED KNOWLEDGE, that is, information that does not currently have a use. It is the part of us that appears RESERVED, not willing to do or say certain things. And it is a facet that can be SECRETIVE, holding something back from others.

The Chest is composed principally of the Stars of Change and Reaching, and it lies in the House of The Motion (III). The Chest is expressing "I RELATE" through the energies of ADJUSTING and REACHING, and it is the former energy that helps keep the lid on the energy of the latter. The Chest is also an expression of the Sea of Birth (III).

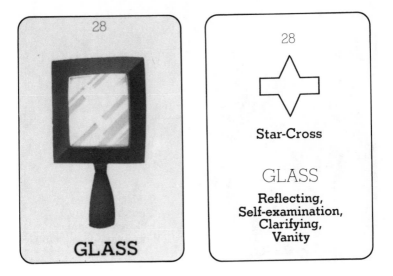

28. The GLASS

The Glass (or mirror) is a symbol of our introspective side. It represents REFLECTION about who we are and what we are about. It is SELF-EXAMINATION, pondering our own motives, purposes and behavior. The Glass can be a tool for CLARIFYING what we are all about, but the process can easily be seen as a kind of self-preoccupation or VANITY.

The Glass is composed primarily of the Stars of Inwardness and Change, and it lies in the House of The Pure Water (IV). Therefore, the Glass is expressing "I FEEL" through the energies of INTERNALIZING and ADJUSTING. It is also an expression of the Sea of Magic (IV).

29. The DUCK

The Duck describes the part of ourselves that is CONVEN-TIONAL, going along with the way things are. To do so is to go with the grain, not against it, and so the Duck symbolizes a kind of NATURALNESS, being in step. It shows a SENSE OF HUMOR, that life does not have to be all seriousness. This same part of us can show SELF-DOUBTS, a nagging about one's own originality. It can also be SELF-EFFACING, doing things more for the sake of "the team" than for itself.

The Duck is composed principally of the Stars of Laugh and Inwardness, and it lies in the House of The Spirit Incarnate (V). Therefore, The Duck is expressing "I PROJECT" through the energies of EXTERNALIZING and INTERNALIZING. It is also an expression of the Sea of Laughing Hats (V).

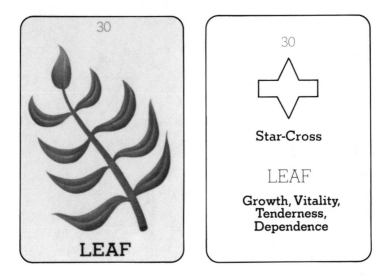

30. The LEAF

The Leaf symbolizes the part of us that develops and increases; it is new GROWTH, beyond what we were. Here, we exhibit VITALITY, a renewed spirit in our endeavors. It is also the TENDERNESS which accompanies a new shoot or budding blossom. And, there is a DEPENDENCE on those things that nurtured the new growth.

The Leaf is composed primarily of the Stars of Bowing and Laugh, and it lies in the House of The Grand Plan (VI). Therefore, the Leaf is expressing "I BECOME" through the energies of INTEGRATING and EXTERNALIZING. It is also an expression of the Sea of Kings (VI).

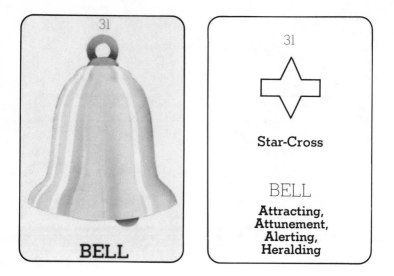

Star-Cross

BELL

**Attracting,
Attunement,
Alerting,
Heralding**

31. The BELL

The Bell is about the part of us that is in tune with our world. Its own harmonizing is ATTRACTING, drawing others to it. It is ATTUNING, that is, vibrating between its sound and the other sounds around it, resonating to a common chord. The Bell calls. It is a side of us that can be ALERTING, warning of a danger, or HERALDING, announcing a significant arrival.

The Bell is composed principally of the Stars of Indecision and Bowing, and it lies in the House of The Perfect Union (VII). The role of the Bell is expressing "I INTERACT" through the energies of WEIGHING and INTEGRATING. It is also an expression of the Sea of Music (VII).

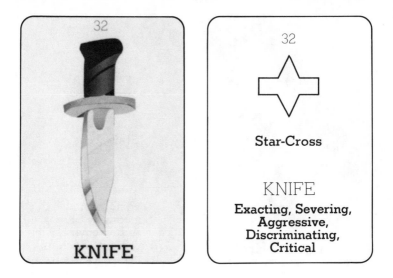

Star-Cross

KNIFE

Exacting, Severing,
Aggressive,
Discriminating,
Critical

KNIFE

32. The KNIFE

The Knife describes our critical side, where we find ourselves EXACTING about every detail, SEVERING ourselves from what does not suit us, and AGGRESSIVE in our posture toward others. The Knife represents expressing our DISCRIMINATING nature, our ability to be CRITICAL of others as well as ourselves. Here is the potential of being one's own worst enemy as a result of hard-lined stances.

The Knife is composed primarily of the Stars of Hope and Indecision, and it lies in the House of The Power (VIII). Therefore, the Knife is expressing "I CARE" through the energies of TRUSTING and WEIGHING. It is also an expression of the Sea of Pyramids (VIII).

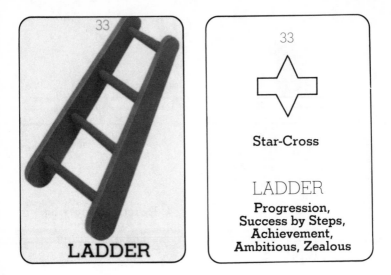

33. The LADDER

The Ladder symbolizes the part of ourselves that seeks achievement. Here, we look for progress, the PROGRESSION of events or circumstances. It is a forward-moving image of SUCCESS BY STEPS, moving up the ladder. As the nature of ACHIEVEMENT, the Ladder can serve as host to AMBITION, the need to get ahead, spiked by a ZEALOUSNESS in the pursuit of personal goals.

The Ladder is composed principally of the Stars of Austerity and Hope, and it lies in the House of The Illumination (IX). Therefore, the Ladder is expressing "I REALIZE" through the energies of PERCEIVING and TRUSTING. It is also an expression of the Sea of Labyrinths (IX).

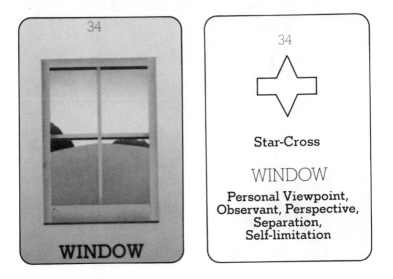

Star-Cross

WINDOW

Personal Viewpoint,
Observant, Perspective,
Separation,
Self-limitation

34. The WINDOW

The Window is about the side of ourselves that exhibits perspective. The Window represents one's PERSONAL VIEWPOINT that is expressed to others. It is a side that is OBSERVANT, trying to take it all in, in order to have PERSPECTIVE. The Window also describes a SEPARATION from the rest of the world, and the SELF-LIMITATION that can result from separateness.

The Window is composed primarily of the Stars of Independence and Austerity, and it lies in the House of The Perfect Form (X). Therefore, the Window is expressing "I PERFECT" through the energies of FREEING and PERCEIVING. It is also an expression of the Sea of Quiet Flowers (X).

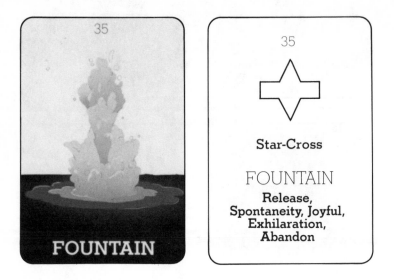

35. The FOUNTAIN

The Fountain describes the joyful side of ourselves, which runs free and is self-inspired. It is RELEASE from tensions and worries, free to show SPONTANEITY of being, responding to life moment by moment. It is JOYFUL, a side that is filled with EXHILARATION, ready to do anything. The Fountain can also be ABANDON, a pre-occupation with fun and a willful neglect of responsibility.

The Fountain is composed principally of the Stars of Aspiration and Independence, and it lies in the House of The Unification (XI). Therefore, the Fountain expresses "I EXPAND" through the energies of DISCOVERING and FREEING. It is also an expression of the Sea of Stars Within (XI).

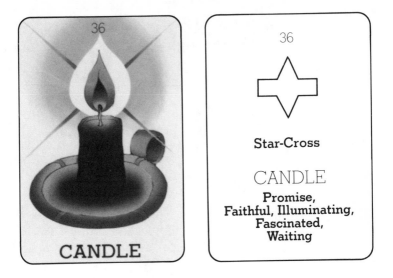

36. The CANDLE

The Candle symbolizes the dedicated part of ourselves. It is PROMISE of the results and fruits to come. It is FAITHFUL to long-range affairs, plans and goals. Its steady light is not great but constantly ILLUMINATING. The Candle is also watching the course of life with a FASCINATED gaze. And, too, it is passive, WAITING for events to shape the future.

The Candle is composed primarily of the Stars of Patience and Aspiration, and it lies in the House of The Dissolution (XII). Therefore, the Candle is expressing "I MERGE" through the energies of IMAGINING and DISCOVERING. It is also an expression of the Sea of Dreams (XII).

THE GIFT CARDS — TALENTS
37 through 48

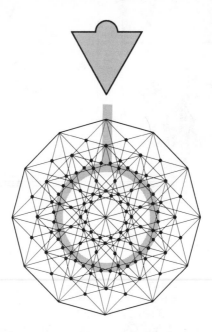

The Gift cards are Essences of Consciousness, representing talents, qualities, gifts of our essential nature which we bring to the world. These are some of the brightest, most vital facets of Self, facets that each of us has in full complement. The gifts are not expressed as specific skills but as the underlying urge or inclination that may be exhibited in a variety of skills depending on the style of the individual.

Each Gift card has two (in one case three) steps, expressed by two words or phrases. The first word is the essential quality, which taken by itself could be overemphasized and thereby yield little of value. The second word describes the ability that can be achieved when the quality is brought out of oneself and developed in the world.

On the Circle Pattern, the ring of Gifts lies just within the ring of Star-cross points. There is one Gift in the center of the upper half of each Garden area. It is notable that the Gifts, being Essences of Consciousness, are the only points on the Circle where all three colors of lines — blue, green and yellow — intersect; Gifts are a part of all levels of the Circle.

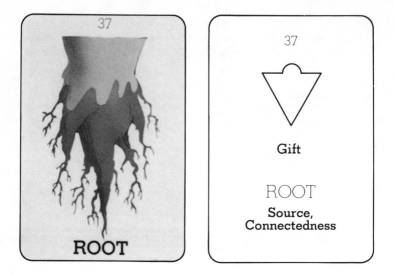

37. The ROOT

The Root is in the House of The First Cause (I) and is the Gift of "I AM." The Root, then, symbolizes the gift of the emergence of anything — that it has a SOURCE, a home from which it came. Not only is this a symbol of an ultimate source, but also of having a heritage. This is the quality of feeling rooted, connected in time. This Gift's further achievement is CONNECTEDNESS, of being able to foster rootedness with others, of being able to make others feel comfortable and not estranged.

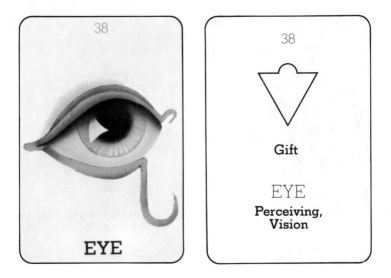

38. The EYE

The Eye is in the House of The Matrix (II) and is the Gift of "I WANT." The most ageless of symbols, it represents the simple yet profound gift of seeing. This establishes the basic construct of an existence. The Gift of PERCEIVING requires a seer and the seen, and speculation on who is the seer is a lifelong journey. Nevertheless, perceiving is that gift which opens the world to us, so that it may be known. VISION is a quality beyond perception — the gaze that looks into things, both physical and non-physical, in order to truly *know*.

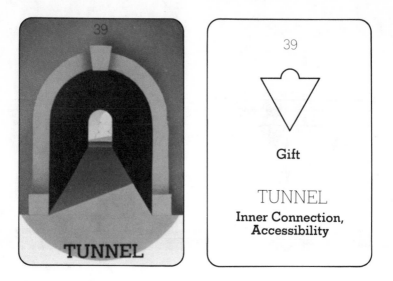

39. The TUNNEL

The Tunnel is in the House of The Motion (III) and is the Gift of "I RELATE." This Gift is the product of the first two (37 and 38), resulting in the ability to connect, inwardly and outwardly. The Tunnel as INNER CONNECTION uses connectedness and vision to "tunnel" within, tapping inner resources to assist in existence. ACCESSIBILITY is the same talent focused outwardly, allowing others access to the self.

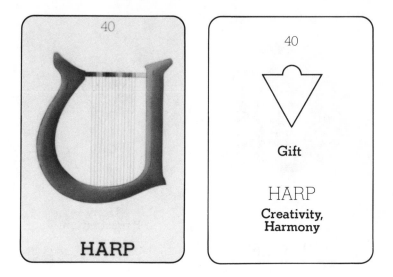

40. The HARP

The Harp is in the House of The Pure Water (IV) and is the Gift of "I FEEL." It is the Gift of CREATIVITY in general, of being able to bring out, to give, what you feel. To express is one thing, to make a music of expression is still another. The achievement of this gift, then, is HARMONY, to make a music that is heard as beautifully as it was conceived.

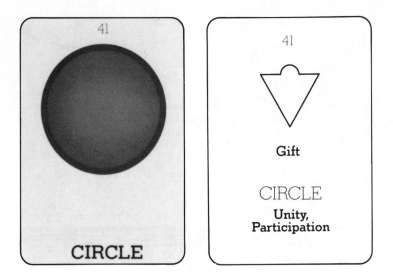

41. The CIRCLE

The Circle is in the House of The Spirit Incarnate (V) and is the Gift of "I PROJECT." It is the Gift of togetherness. If I am to project myself, there is nothing I would like more than to be in good company. The Circle is UNITY, the commonality of all things, all a part of a whole, and that Gift's achievement in the world is PARTICIPATION, every person acting like part of the whole.

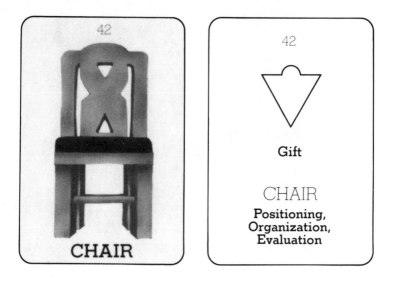

42. The CHAIR

The Chair is in the House of The Grand Plan (VI) and is the Gift of "I BECOME." This is the Gift of finding the right place. The Chair as POSITIONING is a sense of where things belong (for you). It is like walking into a room you have never seen before and knowing right away where you want to sit. This sense of what is appropriate can be brought out as a talent for ORGANIZATION and for EVALUATION, not in the methodical sense but more of an instant recognition of workings.

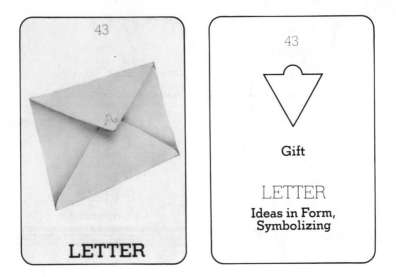

LETTER

Gift

LETTER

Ideas in Form,
Symbolizing

43. The LETTER

The Letter is in the House of The Perfect Union (VII) and is the Gift of "I INTERACT." This is the Gift of meaning within expression. Like a letter, the essential quality is the ability to express IDEAS IN FORM, that is, to translate thoughts into a medium. The translation is never perfect, though, due to the limits of the medium. So, the real achievement of this Gift is SYMBOLIZING. This is the ability to imbue the translated ideas with meaning, so that the message reaches *through* the medium to the perceiver.

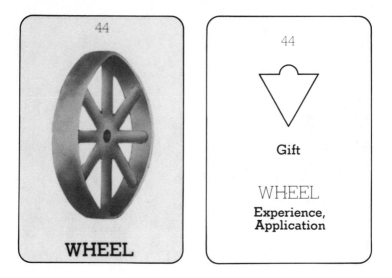

44. The WHEEL

The Wheel is in the House of The Power (VIII) and is the Gift of "I CARE." It is the Gift of getting your feet wet, of going through with things; the Gift of EXPERIENCE. It is the ability to go along with life and learn from it. The result of this is APPLICATION, knowing better what to do next time, having firsthand knowledge that can be applied in new ways.

45. The WING

The Wing is in the House of The Illumination (IX) and is the Gift of "I REALIZE." The Gift of illumination is, truly, INSPIRATION, opening to all the potentials and possibilities that exist within us. This ability fully developed becomes LIBERATION; I see how free I really am, and I want others to have their freedom, too.

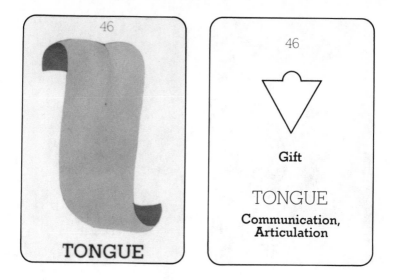

46. The TONGUE

The Tongue lies in the House of The Perfect Form (X) and is the Gift of "I PERFECT." It is the Gift of actually getting something across — COMMUNICATION. The symbol of the Letter has to do with, say, finding the words. The Tongue has to do with finding the right words for the person you are talking to. So to bring out this most basic of gifts, we learn the fine art of ARTICULATION, to be clear.

47. The MORNING

The Morning lies in the House of The Unification (XI) and is the Gift of "I EXPAND." It is the Gift of a "fresh start tomorrow." The Morning as AWAKENING is our inherent ability to take a fresh look at things, whether after a night's rest or in the midst of deepest frustration, and realize there is another, simpler way to look at things. It is a non-rational gift of perspective that has saved more than one life. And it is an ability that breeds RENEWAL; let's try again, tomorrow's another day...

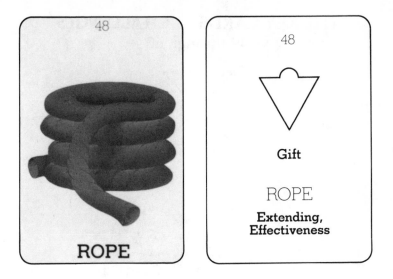

ROPE

Gift

ROPE

Extending,
Effectiveness

48. The ROPE

The Rope lies in the House of The Dissolution (XII) and is the Gift of "I MERGE." This is not, repeat *not*, the rope you hang yourself with. It is the Gift of EXTENDING, reaching out to others, the desire we have to assist, to go beyond ourselves. And its finest achievement is EFFECTIVENESS, finding out how to extend yourself in ways that work, for you and for others.

THE KEY CARDS — CHALLENGES
49 through 60

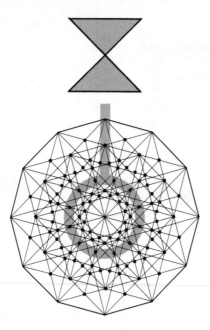

The Key cards, or Aspects of Realization, are a progression of challenges about inner and outer existence. How we are on the inside shapes what happens on the outside. How we deal with what occurs is the challenge. If we have actually created it, how do we treat it? Are we positive or negative? If we don't like what happens, can we accept responsibility for it? Can we take advantage of life's challenges, *transform* our perspective, and achieve realizations about ourselves and life?

Each Key card has four words associated with it. These are like a barometer against which we can measure our ability to address the particular challenge presented. The first two words on the card typically describe the apparent negative aspect of the symbol by which we tend to feel at the mercy of something. But when we can see what the symbol actually has to offer and how we can use it, then we cross the line. We begin to transform it into something positive and beneficial. So the last two words refer to the other side of the coin, to how the symbol can be transformed, *in terms of our perception*, into a realization. In each case, the challenge is to realize the power of personal perception, then to make real what is possible. Because the Keys refer to a process, both the words "challenge" and "realization" are used to describe them.

On the Circle Pattern, the ring of purple Key points lies just within the ring of Gifts and outside the ring of Gates. The Key point lies at the center of the figure-eight shape of the Garden area. It represents the place where the inner and outer world meet, where our inner outlook confronts the material world.

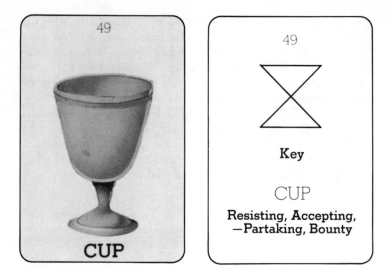

49. The CUP

The Cup lies in the House of The First Cause (I), and it is the challenge of "I AM." It is the realization about ownership; what I get in life does indeed belong to me. The Cup symbolizes how we deal with our lot, the cards we're dealt, our cup in life. I can RESIST the cup that comes to me, try to refuse it, accept no responsibility for it. Or, I can passively ACCEPT my cup but worry about what is in it, feel victimized by it, even complain about it.

I can, though, cross the line of perception and see the Cup from a different point of view. I can PARTAKE of it. I brought it to myself; it must hold something especially for me. I can be nourished by it. Finally, fully meeting the challenge, I can turn my cup into BOUNTY. My cup is always there because I am creating it. What it holds is a bountiful return on what I am, on how I am being at any point in time.

The Cup is also the realization associated with the Seas of Dreams and Time (XII and I).

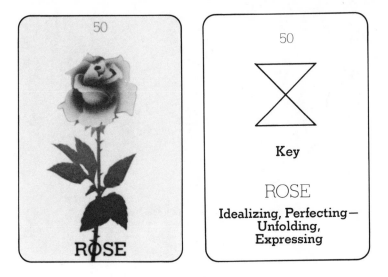

50. The ROSE

The Rose lies in the House of The Matrix (II) and is the realization of "I WANT." It represents the dilemma between *what* I want, *how* I want it and the way things just are. The challenge is to realize the beauty of what is, and to be in step with the process of becoming.

The Rose is the question about perfection, about my inner sense of how things are *supposed to be*. When I am IDEALIZING, I am in a fantasy world of utter-perfection-according-to-me. I can't even really see you because you don't fit the fantasy. Or, I can be a little more realistic. Now, I'm only PERFECTING. You could be better; let me show you what's wrong. The trouble is, inside me, I'm not perfect. So, everything that is not perfect in me, I end up seeing as imperfection in the world, and in you.

(continued)

(continued)

I can choose to see all this another way. I can see the whole thing as UNFOLDING, never quite perfect but always getting better. I can even see you in this new light. After all, you are dealing with your own sense of perfection, too. Better yet, I can let go of the idea of my being perfect and relax into EXPRESSING who I am and how I like things to be. Just being can be its own perfection, even if it's beyond me. This way, you get to be right, too.

The Rose is also a realization for the Seas of Time and Innocence (I and II).

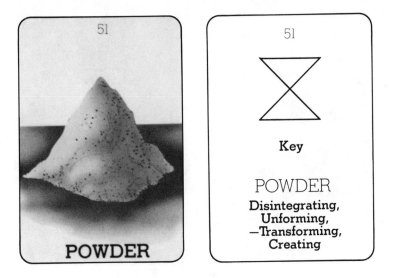

51. The POWDER

The Powder lies in the House of The Motion (III) and is the realization of "I RELATE." It symbolizes the impact of personal power in our existence; we can create, and just as easily destroy. It is the challenge of our treatment of other things, and of the results of that treatment. And, as such, it is the lesson of the responsibility that accompanies that most prized of freedoms — Choice.

Powder can be seen as DISINTEGRATING, our ability to wipe something off the map, or it can be seen as UNFORMING, coming apart, something reduced to its lowest common denominator. In the case of the latter, at least something remains from which something else can be made. We can cross the line into a more positive perception, though, and see almost a magician's Powder which TRANSFORMS. Here we see the maleability of form based on one's approach to it. Finally, we step beyond to the Powder of CREATING, where the stuff of our existence is always the medium for self-expression.

The Powder is also a realization for the Seas of Innocence and Birth (II and III).

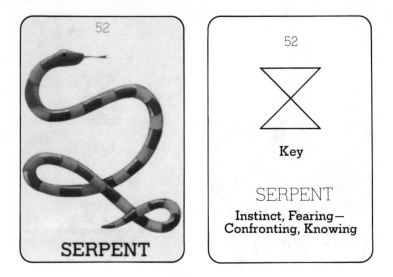

SERPENT

52

Key

SERPENT

Instinct, Fearing—
Confronting, Knowing

52. The SERPENT

The Serpent lies in the House of the The Pure Water (IV) and is the realization of "I FEEL." It represents the dilemma of the developing ego encountering its unknowable source and of confronting the inherent limitations of viewing life from a single point of view. The question of the Serpent is: How do I deal with what I do not know, with what seems beyond my control?

At the difficult end of the spectrum, we see the idea of the Serpent as INSTINCT — forces and mechanisms in the outside world that are acting on us. We can feel locked in an endless game of predator and prey. Inwardly, we can feel subject to our own appetites and drives; they can seem to run our lives. The step away from instinctive behavior is into FEARING. What I do not know and cannot control, I fear. But now, fear steers my course, not I.

I can, though, *turn* on my fear, face what I do not know, look into the eyes of the Mystery. CONFRONTING is *my* choice to change the nature of the game, to look at, to address what I do not comprehend. This leads to KNOWING. Shedding fear, I am no longer separate or out of control. The encounter is awareness, in and of itself.

The Serpent is also the realization for the Seas of Birth and Magic (III and IV).

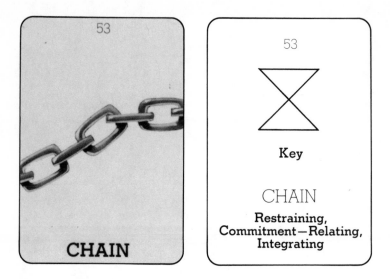

CHAIN

53

Key

CHAIN

Restraining,
Commitment—Relating,
Integrating

53. The CHAIN

The Chain lies in the House of The Spirit Incarnate (V) and is the realization of "I PROJECT." It is the challenge of commitments, of how we deal with the results of projecting ourselves into the world. We make links, ties with others, in order to have a footing for self-expression. The effects of those links is the dilemma presented by the Chain. It concerns more than just our relationships; it is all the ways we make commitments in the search for understanding and agreement.

The Chain can feel RESTRAINING, feeling bound by ties and commitments and wanting to break free. Or, it can represent the hard end of COMMITMENT. *I said I would*, and I will! Even if I hold it against you later.

The other side of the coin is, commitments connect me. We agree, therefore we can agree. The Chain gives me the basis for RELATING to others. A step further brings an even better perspective — INTE-GRATING. You are trying to establish links to the world, and so am I. In that way we are identical, acting like links in a chain. We make our essential links through small commitments, one leading to the next, in order to function in the world. Through the symbol of the Chain, we see our process is intertwined with others, even though we may not always recognize it.

The Chain is also the realization for the Seas of Magic and Laughing Hats (IV and V).

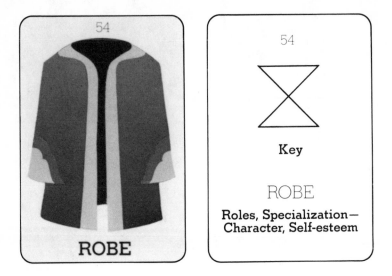

54. The ROBE

The Robe lies in the House of The Grand Plan (VI) and is the realization of "I BECOME." The question is this: Of all that I could do, what will I do, and how will I feel about it? This is not only a symbol of vocation or career, but also of all the ways we adopt roles and the extent to which we find self-esteem in them.

The Robe as ROLES represents our choices of ways to act in situations, whether a momentary role or a thread that runs through a lifetime. Role-playing can compromise the multi-faceted self, yet every situatqn seems to require from us a stance. Out of the many role possibilities comes SPECIALIZATION. Certain roles are emphasized and developed, and we become a cast of characters, each with its special skill (and, perhaps, limitation).

Yet my selection of that cast of characters is unique to me; it reflects my CHARACTER, my style. The more I expose and develop each of those parts of me, the more each facet becomes balanced, well-rounded and integrated within me, and this leads to SELF-ESTEEM. The Robe at its best can be seen as the ability to shepherd each of my roles as though they were my own children — none perfect, all loved.

The Robe is also the realization for the Seas of Laughing Hats and Kings (V and VI).

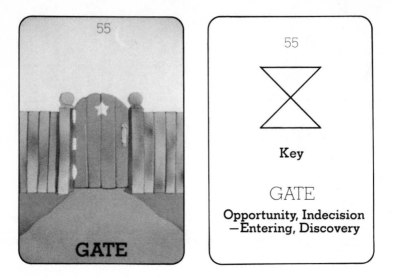

55. The GATE

The Gate lies in the House of the Perfect Union (VII) and is the realization of "I INTERACT." It represents the question of how we deal with opportunity. Presented with the chance to go beyond where we are, we must deal with the not-yet-known, as well as the potential of leaving something behind. The Gate is the challenge of interacting with the environment and with others. The question is this: Will I really go through the door?

Encountering the Gate, we know we have encountered OPPORTUNITY. But, we don't know what is on the other side or where it will lead. We don't know if it is positive or negative, what we will gain or lose. Faced with such questions, we sit in INDECISION, contemplating the pros and cons of what *might* lie beyond. The dilemma remains, and will always remain, until we take one simple deliberate step — ENTERING. We will never know until we do it, and once we do it, everything changes. We are no longer stuck; we are moving into something new and unknown. Beyond that is only DISCOVERY, experiencing what we entered. We will always enlarge our landscape as a result of addressing the challenge of the Gate.

The Gate is also the realization for the Seas of Kings and Music (VI and VII).

WIND

56

Key

WIND

Dispersing, Changing—
Adapting, Directing

56. The WIND

The Wind lies in the House of the Power (VIII) and is the realization of "I CARE." The Wind symbolizes the lesson of give and take. The challenge is one of dealing with exterior forces and energy. To meet the challenge we must learn to shape our caring to the way the world really is.

When the Wind's energy rules and can blow away what I have made, its effect is felt as DISPERSING. When I learn that its effect is not against me, I begin to see its effect as CHANGING and respect the ebb and flow of things. The true changeover occurs when I alter my stance to the Wind and begin ADAPTING. This force outside of me is not going away; I can learn to get along with it, to adapt. Since it is a force, it can be harnassed. I can learn the art of DIRECTING the Wind, using its energy to take me where I want to go, remembering, though, that the essence of the force has not changed — only my approach to it.

The Wind is also the realization for the Seas of Music and Pyramids (VII and VIII).

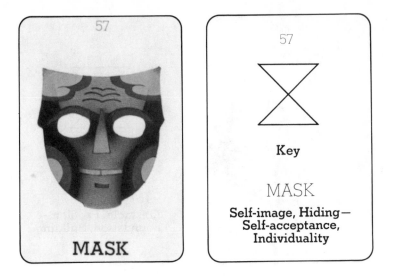

MASK

57

Key

MASK

Self-image, Hiding—
Self-acceptance,
Individuality

57. The MASK

The Mask lies in the Garden House of The Illumination (IX) and is the realization of "I REALIZE." It represents the challenge of discovering who I really *am* and what I *really* think of me.

The Mask is my SELF-IMAGE, the Me I think I am when I look in the mirror *and* when I address you. It is the "clothes" I wear out in the world. But there is more to "me" than that, and sometimes I find that the real me is HIDING behind that facade, unwilling to come forth. Why? Well, I'd like to say it's because I don't trust *you*, but I'm afraid the real reason is that I don't trust those parts of me.

The resolution of the dilemma is to face all of me, what I like and don't like about myself. This leads to SELF-ACCEPTANCE, a different perspective on myself, devoid of inner judgements. Without those judgements, I can perceive my INDIVIDUALITY, and even my own *mask* is a facet of that uniqueness, the unduplicatable me. The process, though, never seems to be quite over.

The Mask is also the realization for the Seas of Pyramids and Labyrinths (VIII and IX).

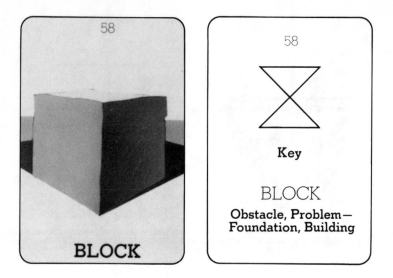

58. The BLOCK

The Block lies in the House of The Perfect Form (X) and is the realization of "I PERFECT." The challenge on the path of perfection is dealing with all the things along the road that get in the way.

The Block perceived as an OBSTACLE stands in my way, stops my forward progress. If I look at the same Block in a slightly different light, it can appear as a PROBLEM. Now it is something that must be figured out, solved, before I can go on.

But I can cross the subtle line of perception and see the Block as FOUNDATION, a footing, a stepping stone. Now the Block is not in my way; it is there to be used. And, further, I can see the Block as BUILDING, something to build with, or blocks as stepping stones ahead of me. The question always is: When is an impediment a pediment? The answer is: When I say so.

The Block is also the realization for the Seas of Labyrinths and Quiet Flowers (IX and X).

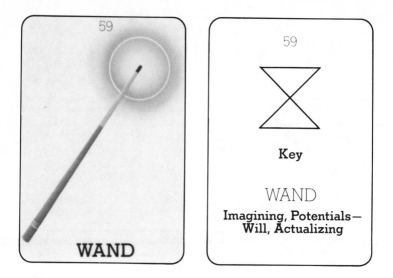

59. The WAND

The Wand lies in the House of The Unification (XI) and is the realization of "I EXPAND." It is the challenge of actually doing something with one's ideas. On the road to wholeness, the closer I get the more my mind swells with promise. The question is: Will I do anything about it? Where is the magic wand?

Therefore, at the beginning the Wand is IMAGINING, and just that — all that could be, if I could just get this thing to operate. Beyond my imaginings is real POTENTIAL. The dreams are valid; they are dreams of better ways and better times, for everyone, not just for me. As in the story of the three wishes, if they were granted, we know we would choose what is beneficial and lasting. Still, caught in POTENTIALS, I can't make this thing work! What's wrong? Why won't someone help me?

The trouble with genuine ideas is this: no one knows what they are made of but me, the person with the great idea. It's not a matter of making the Wand work. The Wand is the symbol of what I must do — WILL the idea into existence. It's my idea. Who can do my idea *for* me? Now the whole problem is turned around. I am AC-TUALIZING, making it happen. The "wand" is me, the instrument for bringing ideas *out* into reality.

The Wand is also the realization for the Seas of Quiet Flowers and Stars Within (X and XI).

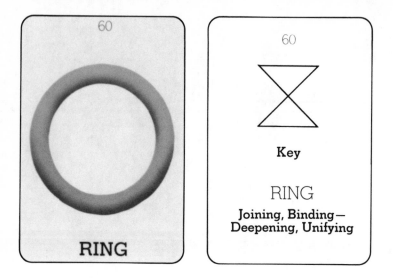

Key

RING

**Joining, Binding—
Deepening, Unifying**

60. The RING

The Ring lies in the House of The Dissolution (XII) and is the realization of "I MERGE." It represents one's transcendence through union with another. Just as our journey will lead to discovering a complete universe within ourselves, so can we discover an equally rich universe within a relationship.

At the outset, the Ring is JOINING, like the ring of matrimony, a ring of friends, a bond. Yet the same Ring can become BINDING over time, or feel limiting, even suffocating at times. How can I overcome those feelings without breaking the Ring?

A relationship is an entity in which I participate. Realizing that I *control* a half of that entity and that I *affect* the other half of it, I can see the situation as an extension of me. I can approach the relationship as a living thing, and treat it accordingly. This is just one way of DEEPENING what the Ring (or relationship) can mean for me. Through this enhanced approach, I can re-unite in the relationship. Now more than joining, I am UNIFYING the entity of which I am a part. In doing so, I am going beyond my personality to care for something larger than myself.

The Ring is also the realization for the Seas of Stars Within and Dreams (XI and XII).

THE GATE CARDS — ATTITUDES
61 through 72

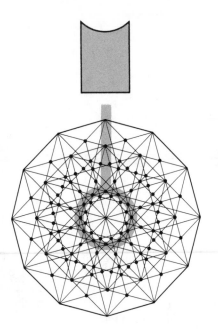

The Gate Cards, or Aspects of Mind, represent the ways we channel and direct energy through inner postures — attitudes, approaches and beliefs. On the Circle Pattern, the ring of Gate points can be seen as the doorways into the Circle's most interior ring, the Hall of Signs with its twelve Sign points. The Gate points are near the base of the Garden structure, and each Gate is shared between two adjacent Houses. They appear to link all the Gardens together around the Circle. In addition, there is a Gate at the base of each Sea area, acting as a way in and out of the Sea. These Aspects of Mind, then, create essential connections throughout the basic areas of the Circle Pattern.

Each Gate card contains two words or phrases that describe its special function within our inner landscape. The words are paired approaches, like two sides of a coin, like a gate that swings in both directions. The important thing to remember about the Gates is that the two words or phrases denote facets that are needed in balance, each requiring the other to maintain harmony. It is the *combination* of approaches that make the symbol a viable Gate, or mind aspect.

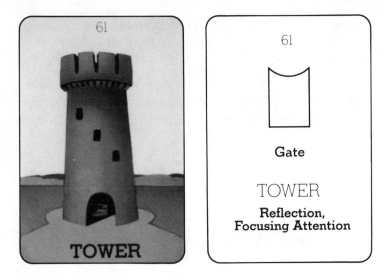

61. The TOWER

The Tower describes a dual aspect of mind that goes with the beginning and ending of the cycle of anything. A tower can be used as a high place from which to view all the surrounding landscape. In this respect, the Tower indicates gaining perspective, what the mind achieves through REFLECTION. This often goes with the ending of a cycle, the mind retreating to where it can see the whole picture and reflect on what has taken place.

From another point of view, the Tower represents FOCUSING ATTENTION, just as a tower can be seen as a single point of focus on the landscape. This is like the beginning of a cycle, with attention placed on something.

The balance desired is between being focused and unfocused. Each has its benefits; together they are harmonized.

The Tower is shared between the twelfth and first Houses and so acts as the gateway of "I MERGE" and "I AM." It is also the Gate to and from the Sea of Dreams (XII).

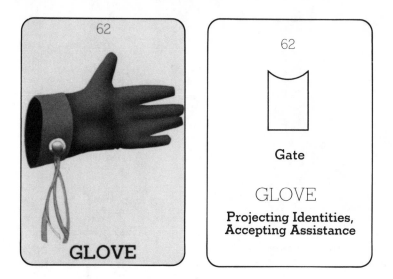

62. The GLOVE

As PROJECTING IDENTITIES, the Glove is making our presence known in the world through the ways we can act. The Glove represents our personal collection of clothes, making ourselves visible through mini-identities that add up to a personality. Balancing this is the other side of the coin, ACCEPTING ASSISTANCE. The hand, once extended through the Glove, is met. The attitude here is one of meeting and receiving the extensions of others, of accepting what is offered for the sake of growth.

The Glove is shared between the first and second Houses and so represents the gateways of "I AM" and "I WANT." It is also the Gate to and from the Sea of Time (I).

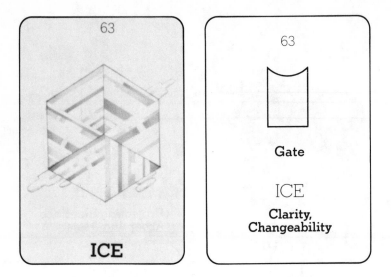

63. The ICE

The Ice symbolizes the CLARITY required to deal simply and effectively with the world. This clearness of mind streamlines one's efforts and dispels confusion. To keep that approach balanced, the Ice also represents CHANGEABILITY, a certain fluidity, knowing that a change of mind does not change the inherent validity of a being, just as ice does not lose its essential nature (water) should it melt. The same kind of clarity can still apply, but one that is tempered by changing climates.

The Ice is shared between the second and third Houses and therefore symbolizes the gateways of "I WANT" and "I RELATE." It is also the Gate to and from the Sea of Innocence (II).

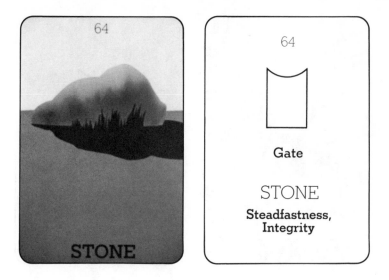

64. The STONE

The Stone represents the STEADFASTNESS of mind that maintains a firm resolve amidst the currents of life flowing around us. To balance what could become sheer bull-headedness, the Stone also symbolizes a sense of inner INTEGRITY on which a firm approach is based. This is the integrity of what feels right within, and of acting in step with the model of oneself, true to an inner guide of how one should be.

The Stone is shared between the third and fourth Houses and so represents the gateways of "I RELATE" and "I FEEL." It is also the Gate to and from the Sea of Birth (III).

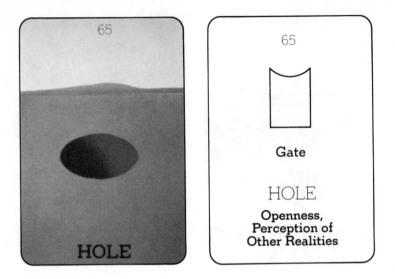

65. The HOLE

The Hole is about being receptive. The approach is one of OPEN-NESS to all that is around you, receptive to the world's input. But balancing this is an inner openness, receiving input from other levels and dimensions of life, allowing PERCEPTION OF OTHER REALITIES beyond the everyday and normal. These approaches in combination lead to seeing the simultaneity of life, the inter-mingling of cause and effect, the wholeness of the moment and the universe at large.

The Hole is shared between the fourth and fifth Houses and therefore symbolizes the gateways of "I FEEL" and "I PROJECT." It is also the Gate to and from the Sea of Magic (IV).

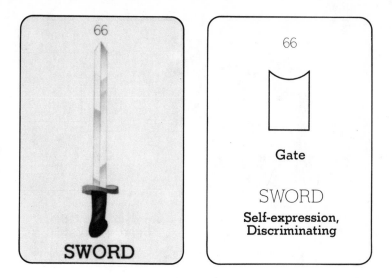

66. The SWORD

The Sword symbolizes an attitude of SELF-EXPRESSION, of demonstrating who we are to the world through our acts. As a sword is an extension of the body, so is all that we do an extension of the self. To maintain balance with expression, the Sword also represents DISCRIMINATION, a sense of what is appropriate and what is not, as well as a sense of timing, an artfulness.

The Sword is shared between the fifth and sixth Houses and so represents the gateways of "I PROJECT" and "I BECOME." It is also the Gate to and from the Sea of Laughing Hats (V).

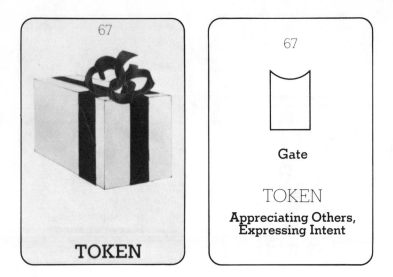

TOKEN

Gate

TOKEN

Appreciating Others, Expressing Intent

67. The TOKEN

The Token is pictured as a nicely wrapped present, symbolizing the attitude of APPRECIATING OTHERS, acknowledging the role of others in your own life. But the Token also is about gesturing in another way, EXPRESSING INTENT. We use tokens and gestures of all kinds to let others know where we are and what we want. In combination, these two approaches are an outflowing of energy that carries information about the giver as well as the receiver.

The Token is shared between the sixth and seventh Houses and therefore symbolizes the gateways of "I BECOME" and "I INTERACT." It is also the Gate to and from the Sea of Kings (VI).

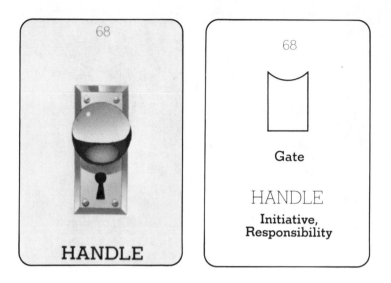

68. The HANDLE

The Handle represents INITIATIVE, grasping opportunities as they come along. This is the attitude of starting things, not waiting for others to do it for you. Balancing this is the approach of RESPONSIBILITY, being responsive to, and responsible about, what comes as a result of initiative. One is reaching for the handle; the other is handling what you get.

The Handle is shared between the seventh and eighth Houses and so symbolizes the gateways of "I INTERACT" and "I CARE." It is also the Gate to and from the Sea of Music (VII).

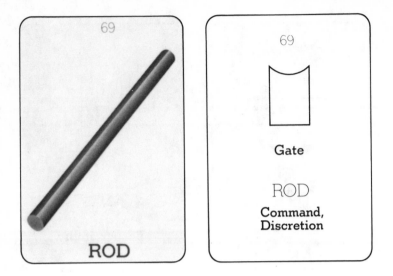

ROD

Gate

ROD

Command,
Discretion

69. The ROD

The Rod is about the force and impact the mind has on the world. When clear and purposeful, it carries the approach of COMMAND in the simplest and most direct sense: by my word, by my will. A compelling thrust beyond debate, above criticism. Yet the Rod can also mete out justice. So the balancing approach is one of discernment about how such command is used, utilizing DISCRETION. In combination, the Rod is the force of the empowered will tempered by a sense of fairness and justice.

The Rod is shared between the eighth and ninth Houses and so symbolizes the gateways of "I CARE" and "I REALIZE." It is also the gate to and from the Sea of Pyramids (VIII).

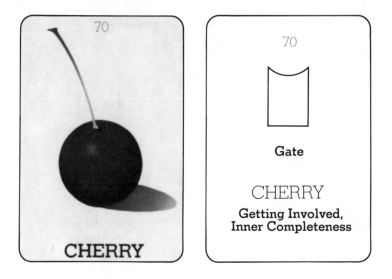

70. The CHERRY

The Cherry symbolizes following one's desires and feelings, allowing GETTING INVOLVED. Through this approach one seeks companionship, nurturing, even gratification. Balancing the approach of involvement is the Cherry as INNER COMPLETENESS, that is, the attitude of already being a complete entity, like a ripened fruit ready for harvest. In combination, seeking out others is balanced by an inner well-being.

The Cherry is shared between the ninth and tenth Houses and so symbolizes the gateways of "I REALIZE" and "I PERFECT." It is also the Gate to and from the Sea of Labyrinths (IX).

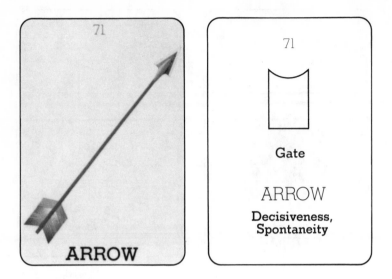

71. The ARROW

The Arrow symbolizes the ability of the mind to show DECISIVENESS, to reach a conclusion, then follow it. This being able to make up your mind is kept from being bogged down by SPONTANEITY. Here is the attitude that you can change your mind as freely as you originally made it up. In combination, the ability to choose and rechoose joins with the skill of steering a steady course of action once a decision has been made.

The Arrow is shared between the tenth and eleventh Houses and so represents the gateways of "I PERFECT" and "I EXPAND." It is also the Gate to and from the Sea of Quiet Flowers (X).

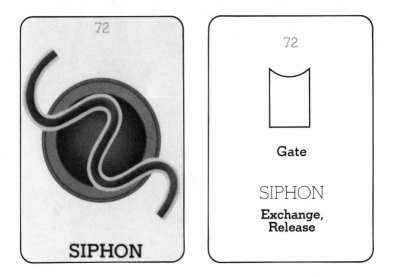

72. The SIPHON

The Siphon is essentially the ability of the mind to let go. As EXCHANGE, the Siphon is the approach of mixing energies with others without concern about the results. It is give and take with no score-keeping. This allows truly combining with others. Along with this, the Siphon also symbolizes RELEASE, simply and truly letting go. This is the attitude of non-attachment, letting everything find its own place and its own level. In combination, the approach of non-attachment brings its own measure of exchanges; exchange need not be parasitic.

The Siphon is shared between the eleventh and twelfth Houses and so represents the gateways of "I EXPAND" and "I MERGE." It is also the Gate to and from the Sea of Stars Within (XI).

THE SIGN CARDS — FULFILLMENT
73 through 84

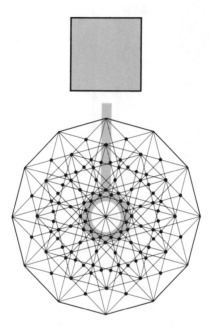

The innermost points on the Circle Pattern are the Sign cards, or Aspects of Fulfillment. This is the core of the area called the Hall of Signs, and the Gates or Aspects of Mind provide access to them on the Circle. Each Sign point lies at the "base" of a Garden; each point represents the inner sense of fulfillment that is related to its House as part of the cycle of growth.

Each Sign describes a way by which fulfillment is experienced. All of the ways described on all the twelve cards are possible for anyone, but we tend to favor certain types according to our own styles and the kind of satisfaction we seek in particular situations.

73. The MOUNTAIN

The Mountain is in the House of The First Cause (I) and represents the fulfillment of "I AM." The goal is one which must be mounted, climbed all the way to the top before one feels satisfied and finished. Such a high and single-minded goal requires PERSEVERANCE to make it to the top. What is difficult about this kind of fulfillment is that nothing short of the top will do. The dedication required sometimes shuts out valuable input along the way. Once at the top, one directed to this type of goal may see another, higher mountain that dwarfs his own.

74. The CAKE

The Cake is in the House of The Matrix (II), and it represents the fulfillment of "I WANT." This is the "goodie" card. To know I've made it, I want all the goodies. This is a tall order calling for MATERIAL REWARD, a return on all investments — with interest — and PHYSICAL SATISFACTION, complete with luxury, comforts and pleasure. The Cake is no subtle hint about human preoccupations, yet each of us seeks our share of comforts and the stability of having resources.

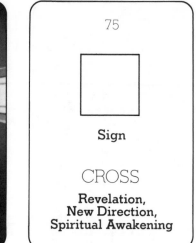

Sign

CROSS

**Revelation,
New Direction,
Spiritual Awakening**

75. The CROSS

The Cross is in the House of The Motion (III), and it symbolizes fulfilling "I RELATE." The epitome of relating to one's existence is the gestalt of the sense of it all — REVELATION. Through such a profound experience, the Cross can open new pathways, providing NEW DIRECTION. This dawning realizaton of the wholeness and living-ness of the universe is, indeed, SPIRITUAL AWAKENING.

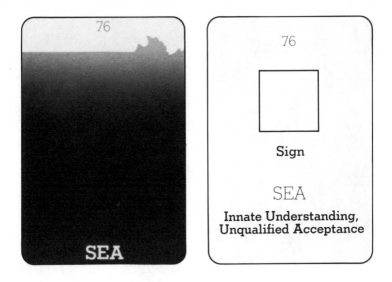

Sign

SEA

**Innate Understanding,
Unqualified Acceptance**

76. The SEA

The Sea is in the House of the Pure Water (IV) and represents the fulfillment of "I FEEL." The Sea, ageless mother of life on earth, symbolizes the state of timeless knowing, INNATE UNDERSTANDING. And, the Sea loves each of her children with UNQUALIFIED ACCEPTANCE. The type of satisfaction demonstrated by the Sea is a complete and utter trust in the way of all things coupled with an unshakeable inner knowing.

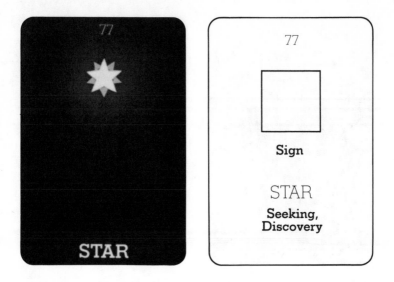

77. The STAR

The Star is in the House of The Spirit Incarnate (V), and it represents the fulfillment of "I PROJECT." This is that lofty brand of fulfillment whereby reaching for the stars, truly SEEKING, results in constant DISCOVERY. The aspiring soul, because it dares to reach and seek the heights, is rewarded with bountiful sights.

Sign

LAMP

Understanding,
Wisdom

78. The LAMP

The Lamp is in the House of The Grand Plan (VI), and it is the fulfillment of "I BECOME." Becoming is the education and development of the self, breeding a conscious UNDERSTANDING about the process of living. The fermentation of that precious fruit is WISDOM, a knowledge that serves as a guide for others on the path of their becoming.

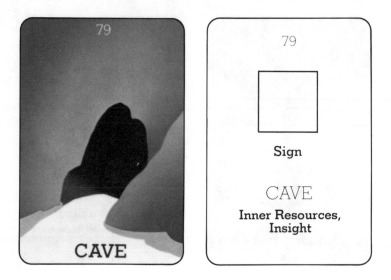

79. The CAVE

The Cave is in the House of The Perfect Union (VII), and it represents the fulfillment of "I INTERACT." The final, the ultimate interaction is within, with the seeming unconscious parts of ourselves. When this union within occurs, we find ourselves with vast INNER RESOURCES that had seemed hidden before. And those inner connections lead to a clearer vision of the world beyond appearances; we discover INSIGHT, obvious and clear.

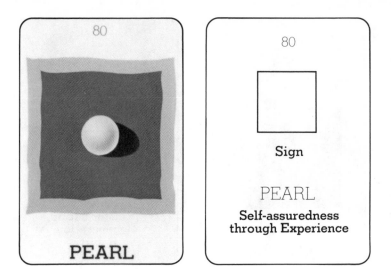

80. The PEARL

The Pearl is in the House of The Power (VIII). It symbolizes the fulfillment of "I CARE." The Pearl is a precious substance formed slowly, day by day, through the process of nature. Here, it is a symbol of enduring the test of time, of profiting from every win or loss, of having been there and back, resulting in a quiet confidence, a SELF-ASSUREDNESS that is gained from EXPERIENCE.

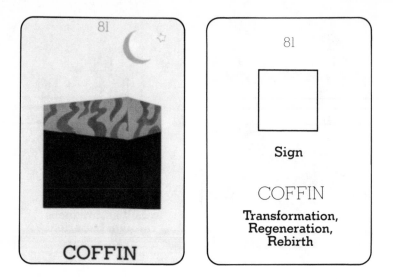

81. The COFFIN

The Coffin is in the House of The Illumination (IX). It represents the fulfillment of "I REALIZE." This is the symbol of shedding skins, of evolving beyond what one has been. It does not literally mean death; it does mean TRANSFORMATION that results from profound realization; REGENERATION, a new life rising out of the old; and REBIRTH, major new starts from giant leaps in awareness. Why the solemn picture of a coffin? The major shifts in consciousness indicated by this card require putting old frameworks truly to bed, but doing so with a reverence for the valid role of the old ways in begetting the new.

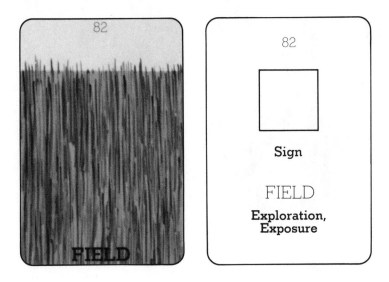

82. The FIELD

The Field is in the House of The Perfect Form (X), and it symbolizes the fulfillment of "I PERFECT." This is the kind of satisfaction that comes from *living out* realizations, for the world's benefit and for your own. It involves EXPLORATION of how concepts, realized within, are actually and literally at work in the everyday world. And, it involves EXPOSURE, letting your true self be seen, *and* in turn, being exposed to the variety of development around you. Fame, toil and service are intertwined in the Field of perfecting.

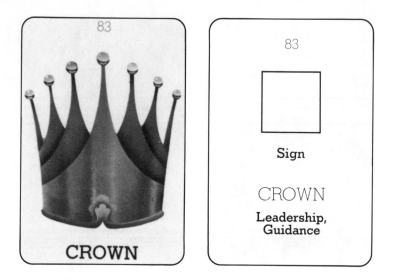

CROWN

Sign

CROWN

Leadership,
Guidance

83. The CROWN

The Crown is in the House of The Unification (XI), and it symbolizes the fulfillment of "I EXPAND." Not the magician's hat nor the general's helmet, the Crown cannot be sought or won. When it comes, it is bestowed; one finds one is wearing it. In proper leadership of my own life, I find I demonstrate LEADERSHIP for others. In pursuit of the right guidance for myself, I find that I convey GUIDANCE to those around me. It is by example that the Crown is earned, and then only for the sake of all concerned.

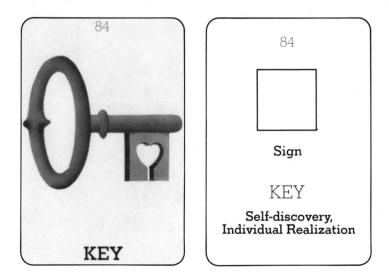

84. The KEY

The Key is in the House of The Dissolution (XII). It symbolizes the final fulfillment, that of "I MERGE." I find the Key and discover that it is me — SELF-DISCOVERY. The microcosm of my self is complete. Perfection is no longer an issue; to know all that I am is what matters. To be all that I can be, INDIVIDUAL REALIZATION is the Key. It opens me to all other selves and their quest. It brings me closer to that grander self from which I came, in which I dwell, for which I expand. I and thee and thou are one. That is the Key.

III
More

CHOOSING CARDS VS. DRAWING THEM

Some people debate the accuracy or meaningfulness of drawing cards from a randomly shuffled deck. To them, it seems arbitrary. It raises philosophical arguments about the nature of reality. For people who have such resistance with STAR+GATE, there is an alternative. You can *choose* your cards, and use STAR+GATE in a way more to your liking. But first, consider these thoughts about why drawing the cards randomly works the way it does.

Divination is the umbrella term for activities done with Tarot cards, the I Ching, and now STAR+GATE. Divination — variously understood to mean fortune-telling, prophesy or intuitive insight. Divination, from *devine* pertaining to god or to be god-like. The trouble is, in the past divining seemed to be the exclusive property of seers and prophets, people who might be perceived by the common person as anything from a messenger of god to a clever faker. The term intuitive insight is probably a more accurate description of divination, and everyone possesses this faculty regardless of its degree of use. Anyone can develop this gift into a powerful tool for living.

Much mystique and superstition has prevailed around the idea of seeing past the moment and beyond appearances. But there is enough known today about the inherent capabilities of man, and enough tools at hand to help develop them, that each person should rightly claim his or her own gift for insight as a basic part of being-ness.

How do you tap into this intuitive insight? Where do you go when you need answers? The answer is: Just about anywhere, *if* you really want an answer. It isn't that simple, of course. Many people, whether they are looking inside themselves or are turning outside for help, find only confusion.

STAR+GATE is a tool for clearing away the confusion. It is based in part on the idea that there is no real dividing line between the inside and the outside, between self and not-self, between you and others. STAR+GATE views the outside world as a mirror, a reflection, of the interior universe. As humans, we live in this flux of impressions and experiences, this constant interchange between inner and outer. STAR+GATE is a carefully conceived mirroring device, based on principles of life itself. When you look into the mirror of

STAR+GATE, you see a symbolic portrait of yourself. This portrait may please you or challenge you or upset you. You may reject it or allow it to inspire you. But the picture is always your own.

Using the Symbolic Cards, you create the picture by connecting events and experiences in your life, much the way pictures are drawn in children's books by connecting dots. The events and experiences often seem unrelated until something triggers the connection, the realization, in your mind. STAR+GATE serves as that trigger. Psychologists call this special connectedness, beyond cause and effect, *synchronicity*, a term first used by Jung. It suggests that the link between apparently unrelated events in your life is you, your understanding, your insight. Only you can give special meaning to these events.

What happens to you in life, then, belongs expressly to you. No one will ever have quite your perspective on the world nor experience things quite like you do. Everything that happens to you is in sychronization with your particular life, and it is all a reflection of you. In every moment, whatever is happening to you is happening just for you. There is a message within what you experience that is for you alone. It may be clear or unclear, lighthearted or profound, heeded or ignored. But the message is there, especially if you are looking for answers.

Since everything is happening in step with your own being, when you shuffle the cards and draw from the deck, it is not random. The order of the cards when you pick up the deck, the certain way you shuffle the cards, the time when you choose to stop shuffling and how you cut the deck — each of these factors is completely unique to the moment and to you. So is the outcome, the cards you draw. They belong to you. They are your portrait and your answer.

If the idea of random cards still makes you uncomfortable, then choose the cards you want. That is, with a specific topic or situation in mind, look through the deck and find the cards you feel are the most appropriate to fill each of the boxes on the Sky spread. Do this on the basis of the picture side of the cards alone.

Once you have all ten boxes filled with a card, look at the entire array on the sheet. See that is an accurate description of the situation from your viewpoint, past, present and future. Now turn the cards over to the word side. Read the words associated with each symbol. Take note that many cards have both positive and negative connotations to consider. Take note also of the different Card Types that occur in the spread, and try to take into account the meaning of them in terms of your topic.

Now turn the cards back to the picture side. Make Picture Stories with the cards as described in the Guide section — Step 4 of the Six-step Process of Interpretation. Try also to make the Best Picture (Step 5 of the Six-step Process).

In the long run, it may not make much difference whether you use random cards or select your own. With selected cards, you may not trigger connections that you weren't already aware of, but your insight, the special meaning you give to events in your life, will play a role in your selection of cards. You may still be surprised at what you see. Drawing or choosing — it doesn't make much difference when your pursuit of truth and real answers is sincere.

THE GOAL SPREAD

The Goal spread is a relatively quick and easy three card array. It provides a way to visualize specific goals and portray the blocks to those goals, and it leads to a plan for getting the desired results.

The spread was originally designed for people who did not like drawing cards randomly from the deck. Therefore it calls for choosing the cards to be used. It is also such a simple spread that no spread sheet is required.

Here are the instructions for the Goal spread:

1. With a specific topic or situation in mind, choose one of the Symbolic Cards from the deck to symbolize your goal, what you want to see happen. Make your selection based on the picture side of the card alone. Place the Goal card out in front of you.

2. Next choose a card that symbolizes what is keeping you from getting the goal. What is the problem, what blocks you from having what you want? Once this card is chosen, place it in front of you just below the Goal card.

3. Choose a third card that symbolizes yourself in the particular situation, something that describes where you are in terms of the Goal and Problem cards. Once chosen, place this card below the other two in front of you.

4. Begin interpreting the cards by turning all three over to the word side. Discover what Card Types are in each position in the spread, and see what this reveals about the idea of Goal, Problem and You in terms of your topic. Also, read the words associated with each symbol, and see how they relate to the positions within the spread.

5. Next make Picture Stories with pairs of cards in the following manner. Place the Goal card with the You card and make a mental picture with these two. Once you can describe what the picture looks like, discover what it is telling you about yourself and your goal. Then place the You card with the Problem. Make a mental picture with these two, and see what it is telling you about yourself and the blocks to success. Then put the Problem and Goal cards together in a mental picture, and see what it says about how the problem interacts with the desired result. Finally,

The Goal Spread

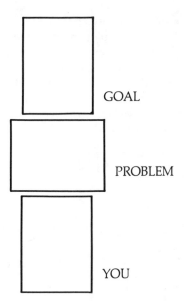

GOAL

PROBLEM

YOU

make a picture story with all three cards together, and discover how they interact when all elements are present. This can be a very telling picture.

6. Now create a Best Picture with the three symbols. Visualize the very best looking picture you can that includes all three elements. Discover what the picture means in terms of your situation. What kinds of action or what new approach does it indicate? This is a symbolic plan of action for dealing with the block and getting to the goal you want.

Interpreting this spread is based on the Six-step Process outlined in the Guide section under Using the Symbolic Cards. You may wish to refer to that section for more detailed information on the Picture Story portion of the process. Also, some people may prefer to draw their cards from the deck rather than choose them, which is quite acceptable.

RELATIONSHIP SPREAD

Here is a spread that two people can use at once. Many people use STAR+GATE to explore relationships of one kind or another, whether it be a love relationship, a family or a business relationship or any other way one can be a partner. The Sky spread is adequate for such topics, but it shows a picture that is based only on the player's *own* perspective. To allow two partners to play at once and for both to have their own perspectives revealed, the following alterations are provided.

1. The Sky spread arrangement is used, but the boxes are renamed for the "A" partner, "B" partner and the two together as shown.

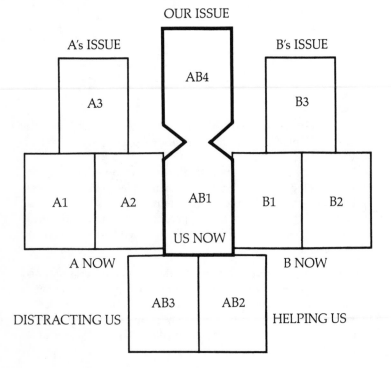

2. The person chosen to be A shuffles and cuts the deck of cards. Draw the first card and place it in the box A1; next card drawn into A2; third card into A3.
3. The person chosen as B then shuffles the deck, cuts, and draws three cards, placing them in B1, B2 and B3.
4. Together A and B partners shuffle, cut and draw the cards for boxes AB1 to AB4. Share the procedure of shuffling and drawing in any way desired.
5. Together A and B interpret their cards using the Six-step Process of Interpretation (See Guide Section Using the Symbolic Cards).
6. Boxes A1 and A2 refer to A's own present, with A's Issue above as a personal focus of attention. B's own boxes are the same for B. For the AB boxes, Us Now describes the two as a couple or as partners, with Our Issue being the current issue they are facing together or their common focus of attention. The Helping and Distracting symbols can belong to either or both; it is up to the players to decide.

The complete Six-step Process is recommended because of what the Picture Story part can reveal, of the sharing required to perform it and because of the value to both people in creating a Best Picture together. This can result in an enhanced approach on the part of both partners that will greatly benefit the relationship.

TALKING ON THE CIRCLE PATTERN

For an interesting experience with STAR+GATE *and* in the art of communication, you can use the Circle Pattern to have a conversation with someone. The conversation will have two related aspects — placing markers on different points on the Circle and using cards that correspond to the marked points as parts of a statement. The result is a conversation comprised of a visual creation on the Circle and a counterpart of meaning from the resulting symbols.

Sit across from the person you are playing with, with the Circle Pattern between you. Have the deck of cards at hand as well as two kinds of markers, such as beads, coins or game markers, that will distinguish your markers from the other player's.

Here's how to play:

1. Decide what you are going to talk about. General or specific, it often helps to have a context established.
2. Each person chooses one kind of marker to mark his or her points on the Circle.
3. One person begins by placing one or more markers on one or more spots on the Circle, wherever desired. The numbers or letters of those points are read, and the corresponding Symbolic Cards are drawn from the deck. These cards are then placed in a group or a row to the side of the Circle Pattern. The person chooses the order of the cards and where and how they are placed. Both the spots marked on the Circle and the arrangement of cards are the person's first statement.
4. The other person responds to the first's statement in the same manner. His or her markers are placed on other spots on the Circle, and corresponding cards are drawn from the deck and arranged in the desired manner as a response to the first statement.
5. The first person then responds by adding more markers on other spots, adding new cards, creating a further statement. The process continues, back and forth, until both people feel the conversation is complete.

6. The selection of spots on the Circle can be made in one of two ways. It can be done visually, according to how things look on the Circle (including the relevance of House areas and Card Type or Level). Or, placement can be based on what cards will result.
7. The players may choose to talk about what the statements mean as they go along, or they may elect to remain silent until the conversation is completed.
8. Determining the meaning of the statements and the overall outcome of the conversation is completely up to the people involved. Proximities, patterns, symmetries, nearnesses and distances, Houses and Card Types (Levels) — all these and other factors can be taken into account. Where and how the cards are arranged also has meaning, and of course the word side of the cards can add other dimensions of understanding.
9. All rules or conventions are left to the players, but it is recommended that basic groundrules be set up before the conversation begins.

IV
THE STORY

From the center of nothingness, from silence, came the voice:

"Hear me,
I am inside you.
Behold what I am
and never be afraid again,
nor ever fear
one thing in thy world.

"I am the seed that has grown you.
You need never fear,
for I am with you,
always,
forever.

"I am the Wings of Heaven,
the Bosom of Love,
the Herald of Truth everlasting.
Yet you cannot see me,
so deep am I within you,
so far spread am I without,
through the multitude,
throughout the universe,
I live throughout all things.

"All lives within my dream,
my eyes, my wonder,
my caring and my loose stroke.
all that has been named,
all that can be known,
all dwells within my silence,
all dwells within my glorious expanse.

"Know always that I am with you.
You shall never
be
alone."

CHILDHOOD NIGHTS

This is the last thing I remember before I was born:

> Three or four of us were standing together talking. We were
> at the edge of a grayish plain. Where the plain ended, there
> seemed to be nothing but a great abyss or void beyond it.
> I was uncomfortable standing as close to the edge as we
> were. The light was gray, like dusk. The others standing
> with me were robed, and I could not see their faces clearly,
> as though they were hooded. They were saying last-minute
> kinds of things, going over things to remember. I don't
> know what the words were. There was just a certain quality
> to what they said. They were trying to sound reassuring,
> almost nonchalant. But I felt there was nothing nonchalant,
> nothing carefree, about this situation. Suddenly something
> pushed me past the edge, and I tumbled into blackness.

I recall nothing after that until I was about three years old. Then
I was gradually aware of remembering that conversation on the gray
plain. The memory, which grew stronger and stronger, seemed to
come from a vast distance away, and it confused me. I was like someone waking from a coma, not knowing what happened before, confused about who and where I was. I have thought a lot about this
over the years and still have no explanation for it, just a vague sense
of having been a part of some last-minute briefing beyond my
understanding.

The memory of that conversation, so abruptly cut short, stayed
with me. It gave me a certain estrangement from my life. I felt aban-
doned, plopped down in a maze without a word or a map. The
people in the conversation, whoever they were, were now hopelessly
out of reach, and the world around me and the life which stretched
before me were a complete mystery. I sensed that before I could
make sense of any of this, I would have to solve the puzzle of where
I was and who I was.

Nights were my time for exploring these themes. Like most
children, I didn't like having to go to bed. I didn't like being taken
to my bedroom and being left alone in my crib in the dark. That
added to my sense of abandonment. My parents, those loving people

who took care of me, made life bearable, but they were unaware of the confusion and questions deep inside me. At night, left alone in my crib, I was again face-to-face with the dilemma of what I was doing here. While wondering about this and trying to fall asleep, I made some key discoveries that helped shape my life and led me, eventually, to STAR+GATE.

Three of those discoveries have stayed with me ever since those early childhood nights. The first discovery was about size, and it made me feel a lot better about my situation. I was looking into the deep gray corner of the room, and suddenly I realized I couldn't tell how big the corner was. I could view it as though it were tiny and I was the biggest thing in the world. Or, I could view the corner as being as large as the whole world, big enough to swallow me up. Its size was up to me, to how I looked at it. It was important to me to see that size was a relative thing, and that it all depended on how I chose to see it.

A second discovery was about space and substance. I was looking at an object across the room one night, a large coffee can perhaps, something that held my toys. The rim of the can and the blackness inside the rim caught my attention. Here I was in a dark room looking at a still darker object, but darker even than that, darkest of all, was the void inside the can. The void was so thoroughly dark it seemed substantial, a black solid in the airy dark of the room. That comforted me, to realize that emptiness had substance if I just viewed it in a certain way. I remember thinking, maybe, then, solid things have emptiness, too. This was an idea to play with, that made sense to me. The idea also made me feel less a stranger in this world. At the same time, it made the world — and living in it — more magical, more exciting to get to know.

The third discovery was something which occurred on many nights throughout my childhood and, in fact, is still with me. I didn't particularly like closing my eyes in bed because my world was even darker that way. But when I did, sometimes I would see the oddest thing. It would start as a little bright speck near the center of my vision, yellowish-green, tiny, and perfectly round. If I focused on it carefully, I would begin to see something brighter inside the dot. The more I looked within it, the larger it became, as though it were coming closer to me. And the brightness inside began to develop, into a light that swirled around in itself. If I could keep my attention steady, unwavering, the swirling ball of light would become clearer and clearer. Something about it was majestic and grand. There was an indescribable precision in the way the light moved upon itself and unfolded, and with it a pleasing sense of its own naturalness and simplicity. It was a marvelous thing to watch, and doing so always made me feel more at ease, more as though *somebody* knew me, my own special situation, and cared about me. In the silence and dark of night, I felt better.

This ball of light was a delicate thing, though. If I looked at it too intensely, it would vanish and I would have to start all over again, with a bright, tiny speck. It took just the right gaze, the right mix of interest, playfulness and a little disregard to get the ball of light to stay, grow bigger, and unfold within itself.

Throughout those early years and off and on during the rest of my life, I have wondered about that light. Could it be an angel or god himself? Could it be a nighttime friend I have created for myself? Is it an idle game? Does everybody have one, or am I the only one? It hasn't seemed important to figure out all the answers. In fact, it has seemed important *not* to know, *not* to limit what it might be. Whatever it is, it has come and gone nightly for years. And it was the perfect backdrop for me when I stumbled on to the Circle Pattern. When I first glimpsed the pattern's outline, the sense of connection through time and through space was the most exhilarating feeling I've ever had.

In my early teens, I began drawing and painting.I did well enough that at age seventeen, with the encouragement of my parents and the help of an older, established artist, I had my first one-man exhibit. Such success was hard for me to handle. It gave me a vastly exaggerated sense of my own importance — in short, a fat head — an attitude I took with me to college, where I studied fine arts. My instructors there quickly let me know they didn't share my view of myself. Our confrontations threw me into a tailspin. Feeling all my life that I had been placed on Earth without proper preparation and explanation, I carried with me a nagging sense of betrayal. It made me bitter and insecure. Now the one talent for which I had shown natural ability was being challenged. Success had made me arrogant; now rejection devastated me. Art, after all, had also betrayed me. I was reminded again of my own limited humanity and my sense of incompleteness.

Those first two years of college were a time of confusion and searching. I tried many different approaches to art, but they all left me unsatisfied. I pursued school and my art major with half a heart, studying just enough to get by. My mind was taken up with the same questions as in my childhood, but they now loomed larger than ever: Why am I here? What is life all about? What am I supposed to be doing? Actually, what I did was stay up nights talking with friends about the nature of people, the world, life, and God. In countless long conversations, we pushed ourselves to deepen our understanding of the universe.

Then in my third year of college, I was forced to take a course in architecture to complete my major. At first it seemed nothing more than a survey of old buildings and monuments, hardly appealing. Gradually, though, I started realizing something new about life. Through architecture, I began to see the sincerity of man's struggle for meaning and understanding. Art, for me, had always emphasized the artist's vision, one person's expression. Architecture seemed to point to a history-long quest for meaning and purpose. It began to dawn on me that I was like many, many others in the world who faced the same questions and issues. In some way, I was like every man, and every man was like me. If I was lost, so were many others. What had seemed like a purposeless life — starting nowhere, aiming nowhere and getting nowhere — suddenly had meaning. In my own way, I was striving for meaning and understanding, and so was everyone else, each in an individual way, each with his or her own abilities and hang-ups.

One day, as I was walking out a doorway into a sunny afternoon, the world and time seemed to stop completely. In that one instant, everything made *perfect sense.* In that moment, I realized that everything I had seen or done or had experienced — all of it — had been *perfectly* planned, choreographed, and staged for me for my own growth. I had always had a choice in what happened, and yet every bit of my life had been for my benefit. A marvelous feeling of insight, of really "getting the point" about things, came over me. I felt a grand sense of cooperation, whether I had been conscious of it or not, between the world at large and myself. Imagine! Each event, each experience, tailored just for me! And the same exquisite arrangement existed for everyone else, regardless of whether they knew it or not.

It seemed a shame that it had taken twenty years for me to glimpse the truth, beauty and magic of living, to forget momentarily the questions of whither and whence to discover my own becoming. Seeing the sense of it all, my grudge against the world faded, and it was gradually replaced by a special sense of purpose which has served as my guide since then. That purpose is to help others arrive at their own understanding about life. I felt everyone deserved to feel the sense of harmony and participation with life which I had realized for myself. Seeing that the design of life is fluid, that we help shape it and within it we are shaped, is to be in step with things. Now it made sense for me to pursue a career building upon this realization and sharing what I found with others.

WHAT EXACTLY HAPPENED

My realization of purpose in life reduced my anxiety. If I was lost, eventually I would be found. Life, and my being in it, was still a huge mystery, but now I was intrigued by the challenge to solve it for myself.

Energy I had put into artistic expression I now channelled into architectural explorations. I designed buildings that were intended as statements about the times and the culture. I doubted, though, that any of them ever would be built. I started looking for other ways to express man's quest — games, models, and systems that had to do with meaning. Each exploration, each creation, took me closer to an idea, that within the game of life there might be found, or created, a game that revealed the nature of life. The idea of hunting for a game about The Game made more sense the more I thought about it. It satisfied my early longing for an explanation or map to help me through life.

i examined some of the games and systems of thought that already existed. I was aware of Tarot and had tried it a few times. I was fascinated by it, but after a few experiences with it I decided it wasn't for me. I had similar feelings about I Ching. I knew it was a good system, but it didn't satisfy me. And so it was with other systems I encountered. None had the quality I was after. This brief review, however, made me realize I had a feeling for what I was seeking, and that feeling was *acting as a guide.* Perhaps I could peer into that feeling, make it larger and clearer, make it unfold and help reveal the goal.

It was the late 1960's, and I was in my last year of college. It was a time in my life and in the life of the country for exploration and experimenting. We drank, we smoked, we tried drugs. Many of us became aware of more than one simple, black-and-white reality in life. Each different state opened a different yet somehow valid perspective on life. I remember thinking: What's the reality of all these realities? What do they have in common? Is there a pattern, a model they are all based on?

Dozing one afternoon, I saw an image in my mind that put things into a context. I saw a circle with myself standing within it, but I was in several places at once. The circle itself looked like a phonograph record, with some concentric rings and other lines, and near the center was a deep, round void. Half dreaming, I realized that the different places where I saw myself standing could represent different states of mind. Each state of mind was just a different place from which to view the rest of the circle. And from any spot within the circle, I could turn and see all of the circle. This image made a simple kind of sense. A feeling of something profound stirred deep within me.

If what I saw in my mind's eye actually applied to how things worked in life, then this could be a very important discovery. I reasoned that if this image was a reflection of life, the whole of life must be visible from any vantage point, including mine. Perhaps then, there were no secrets in the universe, just self-imposed blinders and veils. I also reasoned that what I could see in my mind's eye was just another perspective, a method of gaining insight into the everyday world. The inner world and outer or physical world, I reasoned, must be alike in some fashion — one a reflection of the other. To me, that meant some real model or game must exist in the physical world — just as the mental image existed inside of me — that could reveal truths about life.

Where to begin looking for such a model in the everyday world, I had no idea. I decided to have faith, to trust the way things were working, and to remain open and receptive. It was only a few days later that I found my model in a full-page ad for a book on astrology. The ad, on the back page of the comics section of the Sunday newspaper, showed several of the book's diagrams and illustrations. One diagram was a circle with a series of overlapping triangles which connected the Fire, Earth, Air, and Water signs of the zodiac. Where the triangles crossed over one another, I saw Water crossing Earth, Fire crossing Water, and so on.

All at once I realized that the essentials and dynamics of life could be as simple as the child's game of Rock, Paper and Scissors. This revelation was like seeing a universal chemistry or alchemy occurring before me, based on a simple diagram of natural elements. It dawned on me that, based on what I was seeing, a table of elements could be set up that would convey the essences of life and their ways of interrelating — a table of life that was simple yet complex, like life itself. And although this table would be comprised of elements of the everyday world, like fire and water and so on, it would describe the deep expansive levels of awareness that existence also contains.

It is difficult to convey all the thoughts, impressions and feelings that ran through me in those brief moments of realization. It was a flashing glimpse of what such a system could be, what it could reveal and what it could do for people. I sensed there was an enormous amount of information there for the asking, for anyone who wanted to know. And here I was, the first in line. I was thrilled; it was like finding the Grail at the bottom of the clothes hamper.

The question was, though, what to do with the diagram and all these ideas. I didn't have the slightest idea. I had wanted something like this, believed in the idea, and then found it right under my nose, right here in the physical world. So physical reality wasn't shallow or incomplete after all. Within it were many rich and meaningful things. I could work with it, not feel apart from it. And what had gotten me to this point was trusting in my own feelings, using a hunch or intuition as a guide. That meant that through use of both the rational and intuitive parts of myself I could discover more than I could with either part alone. I felt all the parts of me coming together, each with its own function and each with permission to do its own thing. I was ready to go on the journey, not knowing where it would lead. All I knew was that it felt right, and that would be my guide.

I began that very day working with some drafting equipment. I re-created the diagram from the newspaper and started playing around with it. I was interested in the intersecting triangles, for example where the line from the Fire triangle crossed the one from Water. The sketch that caught my attention was a series of lines that paralleled the lines of the four triangles. As I looked at it, I saw it spin, whirl within itself, unfold yet lead back into itself. I saw it do many things, and it seemed to express much and explain much. Something about it held the same vitality as the swirling mental image from childhood nights. It was only a pencil drawing on a piece of plain yellow paper, but from deep within I knew I had found what I was looking for. In my head, it was another matter — I didn't know what I had.

I mused over the pencil diagram off and on for the rest of the day. Ideas and plans swam around in my head and became a part of my dreams that night. In the morning I bought art supplies to fashion a game board — thin, colored tapes, round stick-on dots, and a nice piece of redwood board.

I translated the sketch onto the game board by what was becoming standard operating procedure, working by intuition. First were the lines that seemed to call for blue tape. These lines swept across the circle dividing it into parts from edge to edge. Next, were a group of lines that seemed to call for green. These lines were like a web and appeared to add a sense of structure to the pattern. Those lines that were left I made in yellow. These seemed to light up the circle, making it appear vibrant and alive. Together, all three colors made a pattern that was pleasing, active, and soothing at the same time. Next, I chose round yellow dots to mark certain intersections within the pattern, places that seemed more important to my eye than others. There were 108 spots when I had marked them all.

The Circle Pattern was complete. I could tell by the way it looked, and I was amazed at what I saw. My feeling was like that of a child who stands back for a moment from his scratching and digging in the sand to discover he has built a castle. It was a majestic thing, and I vowed I would know it and know it well.

There was much to learn from the Pattern, and I spent the next three months almost completely engrossed with it. I wanted to know for myself all the Pattern could reveal about life. There it lay before me, silently inviting me to know it. I had only the barest of guidelines to help me, the original connection with astrology and an inner sense of intuition that had brought me this far in my search.

First, I explored the lines. I named the blue ones Cloud lines. Why? Because it felt right, and I trusted I wasn't crazy and sooner or later I would discover there was a reason for them being called by that name. As I stared at the Pattern, imagining it to be a world in itself, it semed as if these blue lines, in parallel sets, divided the circle into twelve basic areas. Mentally comparing the image to the everyday world, it was as though the clouds and Earth's atmosphere *looked* as they normally do but contained within them a pattern of some sort. So, as I gazed at the Circle Pattern before me, a pattern of basic divisions was etched by these blue Cloud lines. The twelve areas that these lines described I named the Houses, and where they merged toward the circle's center was a thirteenth area which I called the Hall of Signs.

Looking at the green lines, I saw two kinds. There were the ones that ran from close to the circle's edge right to the center of the Pattern. These seemed to in some way contain the essence of each House area; they ran right through each House's center, joining at the Pattern's center. I called these Lineage lines. The other type of green lines spanned the circle's perimeter, linking the Lineage lines through what seemed like the arm-in-arm embrace of a ring of brothers and sisters around the circle. These I named Bridges.

Where the Bridges crossed one another was where the yellow lines emanated. Yellow lines parallelled the angles of both the blue and green lines, but they seemed to do so at a different level. Because they were bright yellow, I decided to call them Star lines. I chose also to name the points of their emanation Star points.

Except for one ring of twelve points, which was the outermost ring on the circle, all of the other points I had marked on the circle fell within the ring of Star points. In fact, they were all on the intersections of yellow Star lines. It looked as though each of the points in a way contained the emanations of the Stars whose lines met at this or that point. It dawned on me that I was beginning to see the fruits of my intuition; there was a method before me for checking my work. And this merits some explanation.

Developing the game, especially at this early stage, was not a simple linear progression of ideas. Instead, it seemed ideas and impressions were going off like firecrackers in every direction in my head, many at the same time. I held each possibility as valid until it panned out or reached a dead end. How was a "game" like this to be played? Were there other important parts of the System I hadn't found yet? What were Star points all about? How many other kinds of points were there, and what were they all about? These and many other lines of thinking were all taking place at the same time over these first intense weeks. Each tentative development affected all the previous choices and those to follow. But gradually the terminology and geography of STAR+GATE came together, like pieces of a puzzle. However, it seemed that several lines of thought were always present, steeping in my mind.

For instance, early on I got the impression there would be two main parts of the game. The Circle Pattern map I was exploring was one, and the other would be symbols related to the map. Working from my original theory that each reality and each viewpoint in a reality contains a vision of the whole, I felt that the objects in our everyday world could be used as simple evocative symbols to describe the essence of this reality and of any other—just as in

Rock, Paper and Scissors—from beneath the atoms to beyond the gods. And, as I worked with the Circle Pattern, as I have described, I was also thinking about the set of symbols—their names, their positions within the circular pattern, and what form these should take to complete the game.

As these ideas congealed, there grew out of the process a method for checking the intuitive work. The entire system might turn out to be insanity or the most accurate thing ever conceived, but it had to make sense within its own context; the system had to be rational, too. So, for instance, if I decided that my "gut feeling" said black would be the color for one spot, the spot exactly opposite it had better be white or there should be a good reason why it was not.

As it turned out, the connection the circle had with astrology and the web of lines and points within the Stars gave me a context for evaluating my work. From a book on astrology I chose the names of the twelve Houses on the circle based on the signs of the zodiac. And from a distillation of several astrological facets, I named the Star points. The former group divided the circle into areas that related to the development of personality and self. The latter described essential energies or types of activity which beings exhibit. By that time I also had a list of simple everyday things (a robe, a chest, a maiden, etc.) which I felt most people would recognize and which were rich in symbolism, full of possible meanings. I went through the list, seeing where each symbol might belong on the circle.

Now there were criteria to help check intuitive impressions. When I thought a symbol name belonged in a particular place, I would also check whether it made sense within the system. For instance, if I thought the Magician should be point #13, I also had to ask myself whether that fit in with it being in the first House (which pertains to basic identity) and whether it was appropriate as a Star-cross type symbol (a type of self-expression). I asked myself whether my idea of a Magician included the specific Stars (activities and energies) that met on the circle at that spot. I questioned whether the name of the symbol met these criteria, how the point got that name, and then I went on to another symbol. The process was a slow one.

As the points were named, I created a simple set of cards (pencil drawings on card stock) to capture the images I had in mind for each. There were 96 cards when I finished, plus twelve more to represent the House areas.

My original discovery of the model was in August, 1968, and by early November I had achieved a complete and useable game. There were now two game boards side by side, one for the Circle Pattern and the other for laying out the cards. I worked out a method for playing the game that went something like this. With a specific topic in mind, I looked at the twelve House cards which were placed around the outside of the Circle. Depending on the nature of the topic, I would select the appropriate House. From that area of the circle, I entered the pattern, placing a wooden marker on a Star point and then moving through the rest of the circle with markers and dice. As I landed on each spot, I drew the corresponding numbered card from the deck and placed it in a relative position on the blank game board. When I was finished moving, I had two boards to interpret for insights into my topic — the markers placed on relative spots on the Circle Pattern and the cards arranged on the other board.

Each time I used it, I was amazed at what I saw. The symbols I received triggered vivid and touching insights about real situations I was dealing with. The feeling was like being at the control board of one's life, a vantage point for seeing things from a clear and true perspective. I didn't receive any pat answers to my questions; the system wasn't set up to do that. What I got instead, through the imagery of symbols, was real perspective; and with that at hand, I could easily see how best to proceed with issues in my life.

At first a hazy concept, my "game" now was a useful and revealing tool. I felt the next step was to share this unusual tool with others.

FIRST PLAYER

Laura, a dear friend, was the first person to try out my creation. Wonderful Laura, whose kitchen table was the hub of music, art and the counterculture in that small northern California college town. She had something that attracted people. I knew that if she liked the game, her friends far and wide would hear about it.

As she looked at the large geometric design on the table, at the piles of markers and dice, and at the stack of cards, it was obvious she thought she was in over her head. She was also in a very spacey mood that day. I told her not to worry; I would show her how to do everything. All she had to do was play along.

"Just think of something you want to know about," I said.

"I can't really think of anything, I mean, unless it's the whole thing."

"The whole thing?" I asked. "You mean your *life*?"

"Yeah, that's what I want to do, look at my whole life. Can we do that? Is that OK?"

"Well, sure, if it's OK with you, Laura," I said.

Off we went. I showed her how to move the dice and markers and where to place the cards. In a few minutes, moving on the circle was finished, and she had an array of cards laid out in front of her. She sat there in silence, looking at the cards as though they were hieroglyphics. She turned to me for answers.

"I don't think I get it," she said. "What's it supposed to mean?"

"I don't know, Laura; whatever it means to you. All I know is you wanted to look at your life, and there it is; that's it."

She sat and looked at the cards some more. I worried that she was just being polite, doing me a favor. I began to feel uncomfortable. Maybe this game was strictly for me. Maybe I should have tried it on someone else. Maybe I was expecting too much, of the game and of Laura.

Then, as I was about to call the whole thing off, her eyes got huge and her mouth dropped open. "Oh, my God. It's all...right ...there!!!"

She saw her entire life spread before her, her truth. Thanks to Laura, I knew right then that I wasn't the only one this system worked for.

Thus began an endless string of evenings, sometimes at Laura's kitchen table, sometimes at my own place. People wanted to see the game, to see for themselves why so-and-so had had such an indescribable experience. There was hardly a night that two or three or more people weren't with me, discovering themselves and the game. This went on from November through the following Spring. During this time, I'm sure a type of aura grew up around the game and myself, ranging from eerie to mystical. People came who were so primed by their friends that they were spooked just walking through the door. Others came to check me out. But mostly, they came to have a special experience, and that's what any willing player got, a special insight into him or her self.

After graduation from college in the spring, I had only one thing on my mind, to make the game available to more people. Marketing it seemed only a matter of getting it into the right hands.

Knowing that the game was a very unusual quantity, I did not do traditional things like approaching game companies. Instead, I aimed at getting support from people in the music scene, where I felt the counterculture was the most successful and prolific. I went to the Beatles' organization (Apple), to another successful English band and to an infamous rock promoter. But in each case, something went wrong, and due to crossed-wires and faulty communication those people never even saw the game. In the meantime, one of the people who had experienced the game, an artist named Frank, asked me to come to Oakland to work with him at a print shop. He said we could pursue the marketing there, maybe even print some of the game parts at his small company.

I took the leap and moved into a flat with Frank. There, the nights were the same, people coming over to see and experience the game. Frank's interest increased too, and he told me how much he wanted to design a set of the game cards some day. I put the idea on hold mentally, because Frank's style of art at the time was that of rock music posters; it didn't seem to fit.

About that time Frank introduced me to Sally who very soon became my wife. Then through some unexpected turns of events, I left the print shop and took a job at the Christmas Seal agency where I was to work for the next eight years. Marketing the game didn't seem timely, and my new marriage and job presented their own challenges.

I continued to work on the game, learning more about it and developing it. I used it for my own guidance and shared it with others, but not as intensely as before. I experimented with many styles and sizes of cards, with new formats and spread arrangements, but it was mainly a hobby.

ENTER THE PSYCHICS

About four years later, in 1974, I started meeting people involved in psychic phenomena and self-exploration. It wasn't sudden, but I definitely started attracting those kinds of people to my life. I met some very zany individuals. Some were communicating with space ships from other worlds, others were talking with dead Indians, one was a Venusian priest relocated in Florida, and with one a psychic reading came with a haircut. There were some real nuts and some very sincere people. The game blossomed in that atmosphere. Anything about it that was esoteric or hard to describe made it all the more appealing.

All this led to another key development in the game. These people, whether they were the teachers or the students, expected a psychic reading from me and my game. Most were accustomed to having a psychic or some authority tell them what was going on or even tell them what to do. When they would look to me for that kind of information, I would just look back at them. They would stare at the cards they received and not trust their own vision to lead them to the answers. On occasion, I would try to help them with interpretation. But just as often, I would get mad at myself for getting sucked into the role of expert. Then I'd say, "Look, what you see in the cards is more important than what I see. After all, you know more about your own life and your own truth than I ever could. Get in touch with yourself."

Well, some did and some didn't. I didn't know how to handle these situations, but in reaction I started working on what has become a key part of the game — words. Some people had a hard time making mental associations with pictures. That was all the cards contained at that time, just a name and a picture on one side and nothing on the other. When I suggested related words to people who were stuck, suddenly they discovered meaningful associations. I decided that if I could give a player a list of words for the cards, his or her task of interpretation might be a lot easier. And with use of the words, the responsibility for interpretation would fall back on the player; where it rightfully belonged.

I sought out several of my friends for help. I deliberately asked different types of people, seeking a variety of ideas and opinions. In all, seven of us embarked on the project — to make a list of seven or eight key words for each of the ninety-six cards. I thought it would take a few weekends. Fourteen months later, after countless sessions which I called controlled arguments, with battered notebooks and frayed pages with doodles, erasures and cross-outs, we finally completed our list of words.

Typed and contained in a thin notebook, the list became an integral part of the game. The game now provided the player with both verbal and visual information. Generally, the new game was a more rewarding experience for more people, and my role was reduced to showing the game, not interpreting it.

Not long after this development, the prospect of marketing the game came up again from some people I met through my job. It didn't work out, but because of the renewed prospect I saw again how exciting and helpful this kind of game could be for people. Perhaps it was time to take it out of the closet and try to get it produced. Maybe it and the world were now ready for each other. Oddly enough, at about that time, Frank showed up in my life again. We had lost touch not long after my marriage and had not spoken to one another in years. He called to ask how I was, and if I was still working on the game. He reiterated his desire to create a set of cards. When we got together, I was amazed to see that he had become a very accomplished artist, specializing in airbrush work, the quality and style of which would be perfect for the game. We struck a tentative arrangement but put it on hold until we could find someone to market the whole package.

Having people recognize financial potential in the game, and seeing Frank again after so many years, made me feel the door to opportunity was opening. I felt something was about to happen.

GETTING PUSHED OVER THE EDGE AGAIN

By now it was 1978, a year which turned out to be full of surprises. It started out innocently enough, with a trip to the movies on New Year's Day.

Recovering from celebrating the new year, my wife and I were looking for something interesting to do with the holiday. We decided to go see the new film *Close Encounters of the Third Kind*. We had stood in line for *Star Wars* last year. We had been somewhat disappointed in that movie, but we thought we'd try this new story about outer space.

Close Encounters involves the arrival of a grand alien culture, of gentle beings whose landing is accompanied by a celebration of lights and sounds, the likes of which live only in dreams. The aliens invite people from all over the world to their party. They do this by implanting the location of the landing area in the minds of all the people who have seen the aliens' ships as the aliens prepared for the final descent. The government, also aware of the impending contact, does its best to keep the whole affair under wraps. The story follows the struggle of the invitees to bring to conscious awareness the information given by the aliens. It also follows their efforts to pierce the governmental cover-up and get to the landing area.

The film reminded me poignantly of my own life, of believing in something and having no real words to convey it, of struggling to materialize an idea even at the expense of appearing the fool, and of sensing the approach of something glorious, and of having a role in it but never knowing exactly the what, where or why of it all. It was my story. Perhaps it is everyone's story in that it reflects the human condition and the miraculous ability we have to surpass it regardless of the odds. The film was one of the most moving experiences in my life. We sat there, as many others did, in a kind of shock after the movie credits had disappeared from the screen.

I went back the next day and saw it again.

Soon after came a surprise. Two months into the year, I was fired from my job. In a major office reorganization, several positions were abolished. My boss tried to be kind, but in a matter of weeks I was to be out.

Getting fired was a jolt, like getting hit right between the eyes. But I knew it was a message. It was "fish or cut bait." It was time to act on my hidden desires or forget them. If I didn't do something about the game now, I never would. I was scared, and I felt cornered. And yet I felt freed from what I had been doing and challenged to take on what I always said I cared about: the game and what it could do for people.

After a great deal of talking to myself, talking with my wife, and talking with friends, I made a decision. One way or another, this was my opportunity to produce the game. If I failed, at least I had tried.

Within a week of that difficult decision came surprise number two. Sally returned home from a doctor's visit to announce that, after ten years of a childless marriage, she was pregnant. It was hard for me to accept the situation. Here was the perfect reason for me not to take the risk. At the same time, it sounded like a challenge *not* to give up. We reviewed our finances, our hopes, and our goals, and decided to proceed with our decision to "go for it."

Now it was time to really plan, to find out what the project would take, to know what we had and what we needed. I called together several friends to talk the whole thing out — Frank, of course, for the artwork for the cards; Ginny, a teacher/counselor, for input on the game's development; Judy, a long-time friend for financial ideas; several others whose interest in the game and whose career directions seemed to fit the needs of the hour. Out of the long evening's pow-wow, it became clear that among us we had many of the talents and resources needed to produce the game. And there were plenty of ideas and leads for getting the things we lacked. I was encouraged but still scared to death. I had never done anything like this before, and I had no idea of where it was headed. Where would we get the money? How would I pay these friends for their contributions of time? Finally, probably out of frustration, Frank said, "The artwork you want me to do — that's 96 paintings and an estimated $12,000 for all the work — I'll do it for $5,000, and you can owe it to me. *Now* what's stopping you?"

"Nothing, I guess," I answered. We all laughed, and I realized that was it. Do it or forget it.

"When can you deliver the art, Frank?" I asked. July was his answer. "Then let's do it."

Out of that meeting grew a team which would launch the game, one way or another. The following nine months were spent preparing that launch, from product development and testing to packaging, to financing the endeavor. Most of the key people involved gave freely of their time, knowing that one day they would be compensated and that one day, because of their efforts, the game would be out in the world. These people gave me tremendous support at a time when I had chosen to proceed on faith. Knowing how risky such a project would be, though, I worked as thoroughly and carefully as possible to avoid the traditional mistakes and natural pitfalls that accompany any kind of self-publishing.

The development that occurred on the game during those months was significant in making it what it is today. After testing the game on consumers, we found the format far too complicated. I was forced to consider breaking the game into two parts, to sell the cards on their own and release Circle Pattern as a separate item later. At the time, it seemed ridiculous to reduce all that went into the game down to a set of cards, and yet it had to be done to make it more accessible to people.

In thinking it through, I realized the word list could be incorporated into the cards, by printing the words on the cards' backs. At first it seemed like an awkward approach, yet the idea fit. We observed that some people were more at home with pictures, others were more at ease with words.

As we tried a prototype deck on the team, a process of interpretation began to develop, a process of turning cards from one side to the other in an organized procedure. My teacher/counselor friend Ginny was a great help in developing the instructions for STAR+GATE's Six Step Process of Interpretation.

About seven spreads had been developed for displaying cards. Except for one, however, we couldn't release them — without also releasing the Circle Pattern. Each spread was based on patterns within the Circle Pattern itself and required the Circle Pattern for generating the arrays of cards. The one exception was the Sky spread, which had been a pattern within the circle which was rather arbitrary. It was the only one of the spreads that could be done with the cards alone, by shuffling and drawing cards straight from the deck. I hoped that this approach and the concept of the game itself would be found of value to people, and that later we could release the more complete version of the game which included all the other spreads.

Despite my reservations, the changes and refinements were making the game easier to understand and use. From our makeshift consumer testing, we observed people coming away from playing the game not only liking it but liking themselves better, too. We were finding acceptance — even from people who didn't go for "that kind of thing." One person, I remember, said, "I never thought looking at a problem could be fun." By now I knew that someday the risking would pay off. Money? Maybe. Validity, credibility, something really new under the sun? Definitely.

TELL ME YOUR NAME

During this period of final development, I went around in circles mentally, trying to find the right name for the game. Such an unusual game or system or method — whatever it was — seemed to defy description with the usual kind of name. Yet trust and intuition had gotten me this far, not-knowing had led to knowing, so I trusted the right name would come in its own time.

Then one day, driving on the freeway, it occurred to me to let the thing name itself. Star and Gate cards were two of the most significant kinds of cards in the deck. Stars represent basic types of activity, and Gates represent mind. Stars and Gates, in the language of the game, succinctly described the human condition — energy of life channelled through the postures of the mind. The terms also described for me a broader idea, that of spirit weaving through form. Stars with Gates equaled people. Stars plus Gates also equaled a universe. It was like an equation — STAR+GATE. My spirits soared. The name was perfect, I thought, although it could be confused with science-fiction, *Star Wars,* and arcade games. It felt right, however, so STAR+GATE would be the name of the game.

That was settled, but there was still a great deal to do to get STAR+GATE published. With my team of friends, I tackled what remained to be done — packaging, manufacturing, writing, testing instructions, and marketing. Each was accomplished through our collective resources, and each required all the skill we could muster. Financing what I was doing was a major hurdle, and it was at the eleventh hour that my father-in-law agreed to loan me enough to produce a test run.

Distribution and marketing were also major challenges, not only because I was a novice but also because STAR+GATE was unusual and did not fit neatly into a category. I was fortunate enough to meet Paul, a product development and marketing consultant. No one should ponder going out on a limb for a bright idea without the advice of an expert who can be honest about your product and candid about marketing challenges. Paul helped me think through situations that would occur down the road so I could solve problems before they arose. It was a tough education, but without it I would have floundered or drowned on many occasions in the months and years ahead.

As the final preparation was being completed on the game, my daughter Meagan was born. Everything was happening at once. My Formica dinette "desk" and antique typewriter were moved out of what was to become the nursery, but my art table remained there where, amidst diapers and baby paraphernalia, I pasted up the artwork for the cards and game box.

A few weeks later, the pieces of the game were delivered from the printer and other suppliers. Cards needed to be collated into decks, sheets needed folding, boxes needed to be set up, and so on. Our garage turned into a warehouse and shipping department. We had a party for all the people involved. They came to celebrate and to assemble the first batch of games. Not even I realized how much work awaited us. The guests walked from table to table throughout two rooms, gathering one card after another into a complete deck — a slow parade, a long march, and gradually tired guests. We were there for hours. Eventually, even though there were a few strained smiles, everyone was proud of the achievement. Seeing the pile of finished boxes grow had its own uplifting effect. STAR+GATE was a reality.

NOW WHAT?

A major hurdle had been crossed. After so many years of dreaming, STAR+GATE existed. Now what lay ahead of me was the challenge of selling it and of learning about the business world in general. Over the next few months, I got an experiential crash-course in marketing and distribution. What had been made, now had to be sold in order for us to succeed.

I would like to tell you that STAR+GATE sold faster than I could ship orders, that investors stood in line to get in on the action, that Parker Brothers fought with Milton Bradley about who would get the rights, but I would be lying. What happened was different, a long, slow period of spurts of activity followed by frustrations — ahead two squares, back one.

From initial orders came numerous re-orders. People liked STAR+GATE and came back for more. People told their friends, and I gradually started getting letters of praise and orders from throughout the world. Clearly, STAR+GATE was gaining acceptance and popularity. Yet the business end of things was just plain tough. The uniqueness of STAR+GATE, and the hard-to-describe experience one had with it, made it a hard sell in a world of fads. Word of mouth was my saving grace. My belief in STAR+GATE was tested often during those first few years.

The stress of running the business strained my marriage, and in 1981 that relationship ended in divorce. Oddly enough, during the same time, I met a business partner, who was to help improve the financial picture and point things toward success. It was a time of grief and undoing, yet a time of starting all over again.

There was yet one more surprise for me during that period of transition. I met Kimberley at one of the workshops on STAR+GATE that I was holding at local bookshops. We got to know each other, and she became a great help to me in both business and personal matters. For the first time in my life, I felt I had met someone who truly understood that gnawing sense of doubt and wonder that I had carried with me since birth. If it is true that two people are "meant for each other," it was apparently true for us. We seemed to share more than just this life. As our love grew, I came to realize that she had also been part of my earliest memory — one of the hooded figures on that gray plain so long ago. With Kimberley,

I felt for the first time a sense of completeness that reaffirmed my belief in an underlying purpose to life.

THE LARGER DREAM

Where did STAR+GATE come from? What is its purpose? I have often been asked these questions by people who have experienced the system. My answers probably haven't been all that satisfying, for I have no clear and simple answers. I know that STAR+GATE is not new, not something I invented. On the other hand, it is not from antiquity, not rediscovered. I have said at different times that STAR+GATE came from the Sunday funnies and from the search of a befuddled artist. Both are true in a way, but I know that the system was not thought up, by me or anyone beyond me.

STAR+GATE is, I believe, timeless or beyond time as we know it. There is a freshness about the pattern and all that flows from it that speaks more, however, of what is to come than of anything else. The system, or "game" — there isn't an adequate word to express STAR+GATE — is a gift, and I know now that, in part, I came to deliver the gift. The questions of where it came from and what its purpose is have been with me since I first discovered the Circle Pattern, the deepest expression of the system. Having spent so many years with it, I have plenty of thoughts about it. But its meaning and use are not up to me but to you, the thousands of people around the world who use it, and the new users still to come. You and they will ultimately be the ones to decide what is to become of it.

I have been delighted and sometimes astonished at the coincidences involving STAR+GATE that have cropped up. In literature, art, and other areas of expression, it appears that like ideas have been on many minds. Those ideas may point to a long-range future for STAR+GATE that is only beginning to emerge. Here are some examples of what I mean:

* Just after the basic game was created, I discovered a lesser known work of Hermann Hesse, *Magister Ludi* subtitled *The Glass Bead Game*. It tells of a culture in which the ruling class are full-time players of a sophisticated game of meaning. On a patterned matrix players place and move colored beads. The meanings associated with the activity are such that a poet and a mathematician could play together, for example, one expressing a subtle nuance of poetic expression and the other under-

standing the same configuration in terms of an elegant mathematical equation. It was a sort of language of languages where many disciplines could be expressed and understood. The simple yet classical set of STAR+GATE symbols, contained within the matrix of the Circle Pattern, presents the same potential.

* Roger Zelazney, a noted science-fiction writer, produced a series of books on the theme of Amber, a place from which Earth and all other realms stemmed. Amber contained a "pattern" that depicted the cosmos. The pattern contained seven veils of energy, each more difficult to penetrate than the last. Only the Princes of Amber could walk the pattern at all, and he who could, commanded the forces of the universe as well as being able to appear at other replicas of the pattern found in other realms. Also, each Prince had a set of symbolic cards which included trumps — portrait cards of the Princes and other members of Amber's Court. By looking intensely at a certain trump, a Prince would gain instant communication with the person pictured; staring harder would teleport him to wherever the person actually was.

* *The Game Players of Zan*, by M.A. Foster, tells of a mutant race of humans living side by side with their counterparts on Earth. They were an experiment that apparently was a dud, producing a simple, agrarian people distinguished only by an odd fascination with a stylized game played by two ruling families. It turns out that their lifestyle is a cover for a powerful game that involves juggling the very forces of nature. The player families, one discovers, have actually been bred as pilots for an evolving interspace vehicle housed in a mountain. The spaceship is so advanced that it has a consciousness of its own which, when evolved enough, will blast away from Earth bearing the new race, their pilots at its helm. Through the delicate interplay of cosmic forces embodied in their "game," the pilots learn how to guide and steer the ship.

* C.G. Jung had on the wall in his bedroom a mandala he used for meditation that had been specially painted for him. I was shown a photo of it by a woman who had visited the Jung home.

It was the STAR+GATE pattern almost line for line. Where it differed ever so slightly, it expressed inner aspects of the Circle Pattern that only I knew about.

* In 1981, I met a woman named Susan through a friend of mine. She took one look at the Circle Pattern and said, "Oh, that's just like Arthur Young's theory of consciousness." She went on to explain how this man's theory, which had been developed over the last twenty years, corresponded to the different levels and divisions within the Pattern. A few weeks later, she invited me to show STAR+GATE to a group that studied personal growth. After showing them the game, a young artist took me aside. She wanted to show me her sketch book. She explained she had been doing studies of circles and dimensions. She flipped through page after page of various drawings of circles and spheres, all done in different, experimental styles. Then she turned to the only sketch that was geometric, and there it was, the Circle Pattern. She had never seen STAR+GATE before, but it was the exact diagram. She was as shocked as I was.

Such parallels and coincidences have occurred increasingly over the years. This is all the more reason why the *Close Encounters* story of a subconscious message moved me so deeply. Whether the movie is seen as a metaphor or taken literally, it seems that something is emerging from within us and that STAR+GATE is a part of it.

STAR+GATE's future role, whatever it may be, will most likely be based on what it already offers us. It is a map and a language — both of which are new to us. The map, the Circle Pattern, the language, the Symbolic Cards — taken together create an organized approach to dealing with the relatively uncharted area of human thoughts and emotions. As the system is used and explored by more people, it may well become a standard for understanding the interplay in life between the physical and non-physical, between consciousness and matter, spirit and form.

Since the Symbolic Cards are simple, everyday symbols, the system is accessible to many. There is nothing esoteric or technical that makes it difficult to learn or use. The meaning of the symbols is left up to the player. This fact not only makes it effective for self-exploration, it also opens up possibilities for its use as a language between people for understanding others and for communicating meaning. Like Hesse's bead game, the Circle Pattern and cards can be used to express the intangibles of living between two or more people (suggestions for this are given later in this book). It is even possible that the symbols could have new meanings assigned to them, musical notes, for example, so that musicians could communicate in their own discipline. The potential could be broadened by adding correspondences from other disciplines. The use of the Circle Pattern along with the cards themselves could also indicate relationships within a discipline that would have additional meaning for the players.

All this merely hints at the possibilities ahead. You yourself may glimpse potentials as you read this. It is all part of a dream that is gradually coming to life. We are each part of the dream and the dreamer of it, too. I trust to you and to life that we will unfold it beautifully, discovering in the end the rich meaning of it all.

THE OTHER PARTS OF STAR+GATE

STAR+GATE
$13.95
(Basic Card Set)

The set includes the 96 two-sided Symbolic Cards, Sky Spread sheet and complete instructions. Explore topics of personal interest. Use in making decisions, solving problems, and expanding relationships. Thoughts and feelings are brought into focus, resulting in vivid insights, new perspectives and a plan of action for attaining goals. Whether used for serious concerns or for fun, STAR+GATE always illuminates life's situations in a positive, constructive manner.

STAR+GATE Circle Pattern $5.95
(Symbolic Map)

This striking, colorful mandala reveals the map of consciousness on which the rest of the system is based. Instructions provide three special techniques for seeing underlying connections among the Symbolic Cards, relationships not visible with the cards alone. Symbols are charted within the Circle's seven Levels of Influence and through twelve stages in the Cycle of Growth. (For use in conjunction with the basic card set.) 15x15," Full Color.

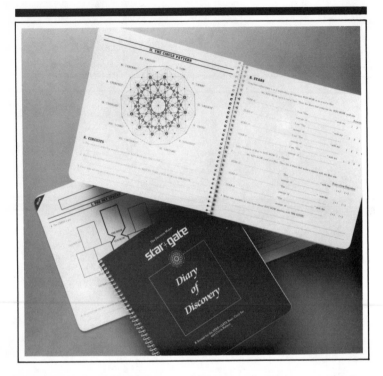

STAR+GATE Diary of Discovery $5.95
(Workbook / Journal)

Diary is the workbook for recording STAR+GATE experiences. The book's format guides the user through key aspects of interpretation. Each six-page section provides space to log cards from the basic set's Sky Spread, map the symbols within the Circle Pattern and record personal insights. The *Diary* includes twelve repeating sections for watching change and progress in all that you explore. (For use in conjunction with the basic set and Circle Pattern.) 84 pp., Softcover, spiral-bound.

STAR+GATE
Deluxe Bookshelf Edition

$29.95

You'll have the comprehensive STAR+GATE package with the deluxe bookshelf edition. For detailed interpretation, the Basic Card Set with Sky Spread combines with the advanced Circle Pattern, printed in four colors on suede-like vinyl. "Keys to the Kingdom" completes this handsome boxed set.

Prices in effect January 1, 1986; subject to change without notice.

PERSONAL PORTRAIT ™
by STAR+GATE

Blending astrology and STAR+GATE symbolism, Personal Portrait begins with your birth date and place to richly illustrate the ten key elements of your personality. Simple imagery of symbolic cards makes every personality facet easy to understand. Each profile includes a written guide and a personalized analysis by a professional commentator.

For details and ordering information, write the publisher:

> StarGate Enterprises
> P.O. Box 1006
> Orinda, CA 94563
> U.S.A.